I

BY THE SAME AUTHOR

1. Zero Degree

2. To Byzantium: A Turkey Travelogue

3. Marginal Man

UNFAITHFULLY YOURS

CHARU NIVEDITA

translated from the Tamil by
GAYATHRI R., T.R. VIVEK
and
SRIRAM SOMASUNDERAM

Zero Degree Publishing

Unfaithfully Yours: ©2018 Charu Nivedita

First Edition: January 2018
By Zero Degree Publishing

ISBN 987-81-936355-6-8

ZDP Title: 7

Logo design: Aditya R.

Zero Degree Publishing
12/7, Bay Line Apartments
2nd Cross Street, R.K. Nagar"
Thiruvanmiyur, Chennai 600041"
Website: www.zerodegreepublishing.com"
E Mail : zerodegreepublishing@gmail.com"
Phone : 88382 91541

Typeset by : Compuprint, Chennai 86.

ACKNOWLEDGEMENTS

Hitherto not published in the original Tamil, these articles were first published in The Asian Age/Dewccan Chronicle, The Times of India, The Hindu, The Economic Times, Swarajya, Asianet Newsable, Scroll, Outlook and Education Insider. Thanks to Sriram who curated this collection. And special thanks to Suparna Sharma (The Asian Age), *Karundhel* Rajesh and Shalin Maria Lawrence.

GENERAL

LOVE, IN PIXELS

The Indian society which remains stubborn and dogmatic, by refusing to accept men and women as equals, has a long way to go in terms of comprehending and experiencing real love. Look at the typical Indian expression of love: a boy fancies a girl but she does not reciprocate the feeling; in fact, she is wary of him because he teases and embarrasses her in front of company. And then one day, the boy crosses all limits and pulls the girl's plaited hair on the street, in front of many people. The girl, mortified, hangs herself.

Thanks to our films, right from his childhood, this boy learns to associate eve-teasing as an expression of love. (In a Tamil movie, the heroine is attracted to the hero because he addresses her as "*di*". Now "*di*" is a suffix you add when conversing with girls you are intimate with. Like the Tanglish phrase *'Why this kolaveri di?'* But if you address a girl who is unfamiliar to you as "di", you're sure to get a lashing from her, verbally or physically. But not all girls dare to do this.)

Technology has contributed largely to the change in the nature of the relationship between a man and a woman. In yesteryears, it was difficult for boys to access pornography. A picture of a nude woman printed on low-quality paper was all they could get their hands on — all you could see was a black, blurry figure and arrive at the conclusion that it was a female by the shadowy outline of her breasts. Sometimes the paper was torn during the ambitious process of figuring out the exact body parts of that black figure. The situation has drastically changed now. Thousands of porn sites are scattered all over the Internet and even a rural boy has access to them.

But back in the '60s, especially in remote towns, the situation was very different, even in co- education schools. Throughout my eleven years of school, I never spoke to a girl. While there was no hard-and-fast rule which specifically stated "don't talk to girls," that we could communicate with a girl, was beyond our thinking. If a bold soul decided to express his feelings, it was in the form of graffiti on the toilet walls — "Pakkirisamy loves Kanchana".

But today, the status of women has transformed. Women have money and freedom. But the dubiety is whether they are happy with it. I see a lot of single women in pubs. And recently, when I was at the "infamous" Sunburn party during my visit to Goa, I saw a girl with two boys. One of the boys spoke to the girl in Tamil: "You didn't cooperate with us in yesterday's 'threesome'… Today it should be perfect. Okay?" The girl replied: "What's this, da? ("*da*" being antonym to "*di*") Don't scream in public… Somebody might hear," The boy replied, "Even if they hear, who's going to understand?"

Media takes pride in portraying women as sex slaves. Vulgar reality television shows, like *Steal Your Girlfriend* and *Splitsvilla*, give us the impression of living in the Middle Ages. Swaziland's King Mswati III selects his wives from maidens who take part in the "Reed dance". He has 14 wives. His father Sobhuza II had 70 wives. There is no difference between them and shows like *Splitsvilla* that treat women as sex slaves.

Hyper-reality, according to Jean Baudrillard, is a condition in which reality is replaced by *simulacra*, which means symbols, signs and likeness. Many couples converse with each other through cyber cafes. The man says he is from America, and the girl says she is in London, when actually, they both are seated in cabins in Noida. The youth of today live in a state of loneliness and void where image becomes everything, replacing reality. This is the reason for the rise in the number of strained relationships between young couples.

Phone sex, I would say, is comparatively better because you can at least hear each other's voices. Anurag Kashyap's *Dev D* is one movie that appealed to me in recent times. Very few films have this post-modern approach. In this movie, a sex worker (played by Kalki Koechlin) indulges in phone sex. The conversation, which goes on in English and French, suddenly turns to Tamil ("Oh… You are Tamil? Then we can continue in Tamil").

If I think of "love" that entices me, omitting this "post-modern love", it brings me memories of movies like *26 Days in the Life of Dostoevsky* (1981*)*. Anatoli Solonitsyn, who acted as Dostoevsky, won the Silver Bear for best actor. Another movie that I am reminded of is *A Dream of*

Passion (1978), which is based on Euripides' play *Medea*. Those who have seen this movie can never forget Melina Mercouri.

Two real-life lovers who interest me the most are Salvador Dali and Gala. Their love story is like an adventure movie. Gala, who was Paul Eluard's wife, fell in love with Dali, who was 10 years her junior, the moment she saw him. Their relationship had some extreme qualities like Dali's phobia of female genitalia and his interest in candaulism and such others. But it was Gala's passionate love for Dali which saved him from madness and early death, just like Anna's love which saved Dostoevsky from neurosis in the Siberian prison camps.

When Gala died, Dali said, "She is not dead, she will never die…" He remarked why it was so in a different situation, "It's mostly with your blood, Gala, that I paint my pictures…"

February 14, 2012

PARIS MUSINGS

Few days ago, I was invited to deliver a lecture by the French Department of the Madras University. The topic was "Paris Musings". Educational institutions give me the jitters since I'm a university dropout. So I addressed the group with whatever popped into my mind instead of following what I had written down — Not once did I glance at my notes though I had carried them with me. The following points are the ones that I missed and would like to share them with you:

The function commenced with the "Tamil Anthem" as it always does in all State Government institutions. I doubt that people of other countries offer prayers to their native tongues like they do here. The irony is that today's ultra-modern youth cannot read or write Tamil because wherever you turn, there are "Oxford" schools which resemble cattle sheds. It is a quirk of fate that a student can finish his schooling and college without learning Tamil, his/her native tongue. In fact, it is à la mode to say that one doesn't know Tamil.

Tamils — no, Indians — have a flair for deifying everything. They erect statues, garland them and then conveniently forget what the fuss was all about. Exasperated by this attitude, Periyar E.V. Ramasamy had many statues bulldozed. However, the Dravidian parties, which adore him, erected his statues and routinely garland and worship them — voila! A post-modern irony.

I recall Structuralists like Roland Barthes and Michel Foucault. Imagine a triangle — a beginning, climax and the sudden end, which is essentially the male sexuality. The top of the triangle is God, Father, Author, Authority etc. There is no adventure in this triangle; somebody gives from the top and you receive it. You are not participating in it. You merely remain a consumer. Now think of a spiral — it symbolizes the female sexuality. The female body does not have a centre like the male body. From head to toe, the female body is like a spiral filled with pleasures. It is endless and multi-orgasmic. Thus, women are more powerful than men — a conclusion which men do not take to kindly. A Post-Modern text can be compared to this spiral, similar to what Roland Barthes affirmed — "The author is dead", which means that the text is open-ended; it's a maze. The reader enters the text through his creativity and creates another text. So, Post-Modernism is against Absolutism. It's democratic.

Half of the population of Paris breathes under the ground (in five-storeyed metros), which was constructed in 1900. Delhi got its Metro in 2002 and Chennai awaits its turn. One thing that about Paris that interested me the most is the "melody of kiss". Parisians hug and kiss each other in public, making one wonder if they are living beings or statues. Not only the young, but people of all ages kiss and hug. I could hear the "melody of kiss" even during the peak hours on the Metro.

"But the population seems to be less when compared to these kisses", I told my friend. He is a Sri Lankan refugee who lives in France. "Nobody can beat us in that matter," he taunted. Like the Tamil comedian Vivek says, "They kiss in public but we piss in public." How true!

L'Etoile is a place in Paris that looks like a star when viewed from an eagle's eye. *L'Etoile* is French for star. *L'Arc de Triomphe*, which is located in its centre, is surrounded by 12 roads. The amazing thing is that the place where the 12 roads meet has no indication — no traffic lights, no police, and yet there are no mishaps.

I adore many French writers, especially Marquis de Sade, George Bataille and George Perec. Marquis de Sade endured 32 years of imprisonment and a long stay in a mental asylum. (Nelson Mandela was in prison for 27 years.) Napolean ordered not to provide pen or paper to Sade. So Sade wrote on tissue paper and published his writings in foreign countries. He wrote quite a lot and many of his works were burnt. In 1810, at 70, Sade was admitted to the Charenton mental hospital where he had a sexual relationship with 13-year-old Madeleine Leclerc, the daughter of an employee at Charenton. This relationship continued till his death, at the age of 74. Whenever I read Sade, a question arises in my mind. If he had stopped writing, he could have lived a royal life (true to his name Marquis), but he ignored that option and chose to breathe his last in the asylum. Now the question is: Was Sade a sadist or a masochist? Even though the Austrian Masoch was born only after Sade died, in my opinion Sade is a masochist. Isn't that an oxymoron?

I am not sure if I can talk about George Bataille in the Indian milieu. One of Bataille's novels, *My Mother*, tells the story of an incestuous relationship between a 17-year-old son and his mother. It was made into a movie starring Isabelle Hupert. I have translated the book into Tamil but haven't yet given it to a publisher, fearing for my life.

Until now, very few lipogrammatic novels have been published. Walter Abish's *Alphabetical Africa* is an interesting one which has words starting only with the letter A in the first chapter and only A and B in the second and so it goes on till Z. The story doesn't end here. He again starts in descending order, from Z. Another writer who has done a stupendous job is the French novelist George Perec. He has written a 311-page novel, *La Disparition*, sans the vowel E which is a gargantuan task in French. And this is not just a gimmick. Disparition means disappearance. Perec's parents were Jews — he was four when his father died in the Second World War and seven when his mother died in a Nazi concentration camp. The Lipogrammatic style was used in his English and Spanish translations too. But unfortunately, my Tamil lipogrammatic novel, *Zero Degree*, without an A and one, was not translated into English lipogrammatically.

P.S. All my visits to France have been in winter, so I could only see the beauties of Paris draped in woolen clothes. Next time, I plan to see them in the summer.

March 4, 2012

IN SEARCH OF SOME HAPPY HOURS

There is a place where men do not get any respect; they call such a place "a pub". On a recent Saturday, I visited one of the famous pubs in Chennai which bluntly announced this outside its entry door: "Stags not allowed." Women, however, did not have such conditions. Well, that was one moment when I felt insulted as a man. One of the VIPs visiting the pub, a stag, assisted in my entry. In India, one needs "recommendation" even to enter a pub.

Once I was inside, I realized that the evening was billed as "Rai Music Night". Youngsters were dancing to the music of Cheb Mami. Listening to his music, I became very nostalgic.

The people of Kabylia (north-eastern part of Algeria) used to be penalized if they spoke in their native tongue, Kabyle, and were forced to speak Arabic, the national language. When they fought for their language and freedom, it was Cheb Hasni who strengthened the struggle with his "Rai music".

Cheb Mami, who was born in 1968, released his first album in 1987 and sold a whopping one lakh copies in Paris alone. However, Algeria's military government banned his music concerts for three years. His wife moved to Paris as another singer, Cheb Hasni, started receiving death threats from religious zealots. Hasni sang about love-making, alcohol and divorce, and would say, "I shall not leave my soil even if I have to lose my life for it." Hasni was just 26 when he was killed in 1994. During his six years of musical life, he released 80 albums. During those days in Paris, if you asked for Hasni's album, the shopkeeper would ask, "Do you want the one that arrived in the morning or the one that arrived in the noon?"

Someday, *Insha Allah*, I will be able to fulfill my desire — to place a rose on Hasni's grave in *Ain-el-Beida*, the place where he now resides.

Recently I had a different experience at a party hosted by the British Deputy High Commissioner to celebrate the Queen's birthday. In a cluster of 300 guests, I knew nobody and nobody knew me except the host, the Deputy High Commissioner Mike Nithavrianakis, who is a friend. But how can the host spend all of his time with me? So I sat on the lawn enjoying a few drinks and the music.

Alright! Arriving at the point. None of the parties I attend in India serve brandy. After a little inquest, I observed that Indians enjoy their whiskey more than brandy. As I am a brandy lover (especially Remy Martin), I stay away from whiskey admirers. You know, Tamils and whiskey are well bonded. If in doubt, look at the numerous bikes parked outside Tamil Nadu's government bars (TASMAC). Most of the people there are drunk by 9 p.m.

There is a joke among the Tamils in Paris about this. Generally, in European countries, driving rules are followed stringently. But the French police are softer and they seldom trouble the public. However, when they find a Tamil driving, they say, "There goes Johnnie Walker!" and check them for drunk driving. The person who told me this was Tamil too, and he said, "This is not racism, some of our people do such things." Thank God! I can't drive, or ride — not even a bicycle!

In February, five men suspected to be involved in two major bank robberies in Chennai were killed in a police encounter. Human rights activists have been crying foul since, questioning the need to kill the suspects. Unfortunately, I cannot support them. The reason being — the artificial democracy in India. Let me give you an example. : Last year, when the DMK Government was in power, a book fair was organized in Madurai. The organizers had placed a few cut-outs of writers there. Suddenly, out of nowhere, a group walked up and began to pick up all the flex board cut-outs carrying a girl's picture. Why? The girl, a daughter of an aide of Azhagiri (son of M. Karunanidhi), had reached "puberty".

Nobody even dared to lift their little finger against these men, not even the human rights activists. Can one call such a country, democratic? Bank robbery and mugging have become daily news. Robbers casually enter houses, kill sleeping people and take away jewellery, cash and other valuables. According to police records, many of the robbers are from northern border states, and most of them are bonded labourers made to work in stone quarries. The police, often unable to control such robberies, become demoralized and this frustration results in impulsive, often deadly, reactions.

One of the reasons why people in cities live with a feeling of insecurity is due to the humongous disparity between the rich and the poor. In many villages of Tamil Nadu, the monthly income of a private school teacher is Rs. 1,000 and for employees at say, petrol bunks is, Rs. 2,000. However, the income of a movie actor is Rs. 20 crore. In such a situation, how can you stop crimes?

Isn't there a stark similarity between the animals that run from the forest into the village in search of food and the bonded labourers who become robbers, even killers?

What is happening here is a war between the haves and the have-nots. And the police think that "everything is fair in war"! Just like my human rights activist friends, I too desire to stand with political correctness. But my conscience refuses.

April 20, 2012

THE STRAY DOG AND I

Louis-Ferdinand Celine is one of the most important writers in French literature. I read his *Journey to the End of the Night* during my college days and it left a deep impact on me. In fact, whenever I read Celine, I cannot help but compare him with Jean Genet.

Genet was not just the darling of the Left but was celebrated by others as well. It is easy to live with political correctness and be rewarded for that. So Genet bagged the "saint" title. Whereas Celine, due to his anti-Semitic view, was marked as a "national disgrace" and was exiled. Life becomes an agony when you are a detested person. Maybe that is precisely the reason why Celine disliked human contact. He lived with half a dozen dogs.

I adore dogs. However, I do not know why most Indians hate dogs. Interestingly, in the Mahabharata, when the Pandavas and Draupadi were making their *yatra* to the Himalayas, they were accompanied by a dog. On their climb towards heaven, one by one, the brothers and Draupadi stumbled to death, unable to bear the exhaustion. Only Yudhisthira and the dog continued their journey. I often envisage Yudhisthira walking in the Himalayas with the dog.

I wonder whether "Saint Bernard" existed during the

times of the Mahabharata. This is the only breed of dog that is called a "saint" and the reason it is revered so, is because it had accompanied the monks traversing the Alps mountains. The poignant 17th-century paintings of Saint Bernard dogs, who rescued people caught in an avalanche, are heart-rending even today.

While Yudhisthira and the dog were sauntering in the Himalayas, Lord Indra arrived in his chariot and said, "Step into the chariot, I shall drop you in heaven." Yudhisthira agreed but then Indra stopped him and said, "Dogs do not have a place in heaven." Yudhisthira replied, "In that case, I do not want heaven." And then the dog disappeared. Dharma had disguised himself as a dog to test Yudhisthira.

Dogs are God's gift to mankind. In Europe, most houses have pets. People who walk their dogs have a piece of cloth and a small bag in their hands. When the dog poops, they duteously pick it up, put it in the bag and move on.

If born as a dog, it should never be as a street dog in an Asian country because they wander in the streets like orphans and are thrown stones at by kids. They have to bear the spit of women when they mate happily around the street corner. Isn't the life of a street dog so impudent?

Anyway, when millions of people are living below the poverty line, why would anyone be worried about dogs?

I have two dogs. One is a Labrador (Pappu) and the other is a Great Dane (Zorro). The two follow me around like two shadows. While I work on my computer, they lie under my legs and when I go to the washroom, they wait for me on the doorstep. Zorro does not spare any place even for my wife in bed whereas Pappu, forgoes and sleeps under the bed. Like humans, dogs are possessive too. When I come back home, they fight with each other to cuddle with me first.

Apart from my pet dogs, I merrily experience the love of stray dogs as well. One such lovable white mongrel, who lived on our street, dashes towards me and leaps up as soon as he sees me, as if we have known each other for ages. I have named him Whitie. Just to repay him for his warmth, I sometimes treat him to biscuits.

Whitie surprised me one morning. My routine is to walk for an hour on the beach road opposite my house, starting at five in the morning. As per usual, I begun walking on that day too, when Whitie, who would normally be asleep under some car at that time, started following me joyfully with his usual jumps. He did not stop at the end of the road as was his custom, but continued following me even after I had walked on to the next road.

Every day I cross the Santhome High Road and pray for a few minutes in the cathedral where the body of St. Thomas is laid to rest and then resume my walk. Only three places in the world have cathedrals raised over the tombs of the apostles of Christ: Basilica of St. Peter in Rome, Cathedral of St. James in Spain, and the third is the cathedral of St. Thomas in Mylapore.

Even at that early hour, the highway was heavy with traffic. Who even notices traffic signals nowadays? We just have to scurry to the other side of the road when there's a lull in the traffic. But Whitie made me anxious and I didn't cross the road for fear of Whitie getting hurt by speeding vehicles. I reached the light house in ten minutes. Now there was no other go but to cross the road if I wanted to take the beach road. I glanced at Whitie. He was looking at me curiously, wagging his tail. I returned home without completing my walk, with Whitie…

June 3, 2012

CHILDREN OF LESSER PARENTS

"Is it surprising that prisons resemble factories, schools, barracks, hospitals, which all resemble prisons?"

- Michel Foucault in *Discipline and Punish*

While there are many people to speak up for women, dalits and other minorities, the children of our country remain voiceless; they have nobody to turn to. The only difference between those oppressed and the children in India is that the kids are smothered in the name of love.

The rush and push starts early, when parents enroll their tiny tots, who have hardly started talking, in schools where loads of knowledge is stuffed into their heads without but not wisdom or values.

The commencement of this academic year in Tamil Nadu was marked by a newspaper headline about the death of schoolchildren. The first news report detailed the death of a small girl who was crushed as she slipped down to the road through a hole in the floor of the bus she was travelling in. The driver was callous. No less so was the transport officer who approved the fitness certificate for this godforsaken vehicle. We often hear of children falling into pits dug for various reasons, and covered carelessly by workers with flimsy materials. But the carelessness or irresponsibility of these workers also has to do with the fact that they are brought from the backward states of India for a meagre daily wage of Rs 300 (for 12 hours of work) like they were slaves. The condition of their working environments do not help matters either. A few days ago, ten workers died when the roof of an engineering college where they were working at, caved in. That was not an accident; it was the result of the people's indifference; the people who treated workers as dispensable beings and urged that the work should be completed at the earliest.

The news of the girl who died slipping through a hole in the bus whipped up a frenzy in Tamil Nadu, but a tragedy is forgotten as subsequent tragedies come along. For example, a few years before, a girl fell into the Cooum river through a huge crack in the Napier Bridge near the Marina Beach. How many local people remember the incident now? The very next day of that bus incident, another child who tried to cross the road after descending from his school bus, was run over by the same bus and died. It is a common sight in Tamil Nadu that several schoolchildren are carried around like cattle in autorickshaws, which are designed to carry only three people.

Every year, students in Belgium go on an educational field trip to the Swiss Alps, and this year, in March, a tourist bus carrying 52 people crashed into a wall inside a tunnel. Twenty-two among the dead, were children. When those white coffins reached Belgium, they were brought into the city from the airport by a military convoy of hearses. The whole of Belgium mourned for them that day. The national flag flew at half-mast, people shut off their vehicles and trains ceased to run for a minute, to mourn the dead. Western countries treat their children as though they were a treasure. If a child looks sad at school, authorities visit their homes to discover the reason.

But here is how we treat our children in this country. This incident happened in what is considered to be a top-notch school in Chennai. Parents would pay any amount of money to get their children a seat at this school. It is said that the school does not accept any "recommendations" and admission into the school is based on merit alone. Last week, a Class four boy drowned in the school's swimming pool. The school, with a pool on its campus, has made it mandatory for students to take up swimming lessons. Apart from the mandatory lessons, the school also scheduled its swimming classes during the first hour of the day without considering the simple fact that it was not advisable to swim on a full stomach. The pool's depth is from two and a half to seven feet. It is a matter of pride for these schools to have swimming classes in their curriculum. This by itself is not a bad idea. But is it also a matter of pride not to have any provision for emergency first-aid, which could have saved the boy?

That was not all. The school handled this situation rather crudely. Even after the boy was declared dead by the doctors at 10 am, the school continued with its classes as per usual, on that day. There was a huge commotion outside the school premises on catching wind of the news, especially since the parents had not been informed about whose child it was for a few petrified hours.

In our country, it's not only the schools that should be blamed but the parents too, who want their children to be Superman. So the schools cater to them, with their "package education" which ensures that the child will be taught swimming, music, dance, cricket, foreign languages, painting, shooting, etc. The kids are seen as grade-obtaining machines and are tormented. The upshot is that private schools have now become commercial joints.

India urgently needs educational reforms lest there be a danger of future generations sinking into an abyss of psychological trauma. I would like to cite two incidents here. One, I was talking to a group of upper-class children aged between 10 and 15. "You perform well in school but I have serious concerns about whether you kids will live happily," I said. "Oh! That's easy uncle. We'll read a big book on 'How to live happily'" came the reply from one of the boys.

One day while I was travelling in an autorickshaw, the car in front of us stopped all of a sudden. So our auto and a lot of other vehicles behind us had to stop as well. The chauffeur got out, came round to the left of the car and opened its rear door to a 15-year-old girl who slowly alighted from the car and sashayed to the temple nearby. The driver reverentially waited until she got to the temple, then closed the door and restarted the car despite the loud horns blaring from all the vehicles behind our autorickshaw.

Somewhere, something is wrong.

July 22, 2012

A fellow writer once remarked that my (Tamil) fans reminded him of Osama bin Laden's followers. He meant their fanaticism. I ignored his comment as I thought him envious - considering the "respect" writers have for each other.

But a recent incident proved my friend's comment right and portrayed a special trait of the Tamils. I have a reader's forum on Facebook, where a fan of mine called Senthil Murugan wrote something which hurt me. He apologized saying that the particular comment was unintentional and he updated his status thus,

"Whenever I'm perturbed, an outing followed by a clean tonsure and a dip in the sea would give me a huge relief. It isn't devotion, but a sort of mental rejuvenation. So I went to Thiruchendur, (The god of Thiruchendur is Senthil Murugan) shaved my head off, making my hair disappear in thirty seconds and stood in my saffron dhoti in warm, chest deep sea water. Then, I removed my last piece of cloth too, wrapped it around my neck, with the sea as my only drape, wondering — 'is this how a child would feel in the mother's womb?'"

I came to my senses when I heard a loud "hey" from a policeman. "Why are you standing there?" He probably thought I was going to drown myself. I scrambled to the shore — of course I restored the cloth around my neck to its right place.

I had this curiosity about a custom of the Tamils — piercing various parts of their bodies with metal rods as a sign of gratitude to God. My interest was whetted when I saw people piercing themselves, after my ablution in a *Nazhi* well. When I admitted my interest to the person who pierces these rods for people, he replied that it was not a joke and I should have vowed to God that I would pierce my body. "Just now I vowed..." Hearing my reply he gave me a once-over and recited the norms and conditions. I accepted, paid and after garlanding me, two metal rods were brought. The priest kneaded my hand like dough for a couple of minutes and struck hard; in a *nano* second, before I could recover from the shock, he pierced the rod into my arm. I felt the pain of the blow more than the pierce. When the process was repeated on the other hand, I thought, "Why view this torment in a negative way?" It strangely comforted me while I was in that depressed state of mind which emerged after a silly comment of mine had hurt my guru. When somebody gets pleasure out of tormenting himself, without hurting others, I think, the torment becomes positive.

Meanwhile, the priest smeared sacred ash on the gash and exclaimed, "He's silent. I think he's in trance! *Arohara*!!"

After killing the asura, when Lord Subramanya performed a puja as an act of atonement, he invoked a sacred watershed called *Skandha Pushkarini*, which is now called the *Nazhi* well. With a width of one square foot, the water of this well tastes sweet despite its location on the beach and it is considered an elixir.

I remember a completely opposite incident. When I had been to an S&M club in Paris, I saw many iron instruments which makes you feel like you have entered an ironsmith's shop.

Torturing oneself for the sake of their beloved is a custom that exists in many cultures though it is more prevalent in Tamil Nadu. Once a journalist invited me to his office to show me a bottle containing a thumb and a letter from the person the thumb was attached to; the letter requested the journalist to deliver that "tribute" to his beloved actor. In another incident, a man chopped off his tongue and tossed it into a temple's "*Hundi*" praying for his leader's victory in the elections.

But when these incidents happen in the life of an artist, it rises to epic proportions. Take the example of Van Gogh cutting his ear off for a girl and Werner Herzog, one of my favourite directors, who walked from Paris to Munich, in the winter of 1974 with just a backpack, when the doctors told him that his friend Lotte Eisner in Paris was terribly sick and counting her days. He had documented his three-week journey in his book *Of Walking in Ice: Munich-Paris 23 November-14 December 1974*. He met Eisner in Paris. She died 10 years later.

December 23, 2006: My friend and I were strolling in Champs Elysées in Paris. I had to leave for Chennai in two days for I was completely broke. I was feeling distraught over the fact that I couldn't stay for the New Year celebration in Champs Elysées. My friend said, "Next time, don't forget to visit Lourdes…" and continued after a pause, "but you can visit only if the revered lady of Lourdes calls you." I vowed to make it to Lourdes, 660 km from Paris, the next time.

The next day, when I was standing near a Tamil bookstore in La Chappelle, a gentleman whom I did not know invited me to his place for a week. When I told him my status, he postponed the date of my departure and sponsored me to stay at his place, in Toulouse, which is close to Lourdes. That Christmas, I was genuflecting at the altar of the Lady of Lourdes. I also brought home the sacred water of Lourdes, which they say has healing powers.

September 16, 2012

Wolf Totem by Jiang Rong has sold a million copies uptil today, not to mention the amount of pirated copies — similar to Mao's *Red Book* in its heyday. I would classify this book under the field of "anthropology" rather than categorize it as literature. This book sets a terrific pace like Oscar Lewis' anthropological book *La Vida*.

There are no fictional elements in the book, and it predominantly contains interview sessions with family members describing their lives. Though it was meant as an anthropological piece of research, the eloquent narration of a life filled with cruelty, violence, carnal lust and perversions, was avidly read by readers, just like they would read a novel. In the wake of the Cultural Revolution, Chen Shen, a young student from Beijing travels to the grasslands of Olonbulag in Inner Mongolia . And he happens to live with the nomadic herders for eleven years before returning to Beijing. *Wolf Totem* illustrates those eleven years at Olonbulag.

No one in history plundered as many nations as Genghis Khan did. He hailed from a nomadic race from one of the least populated regions of the world where the Mongolian language did not even have its own script. Someone from such a primitive culture managed to do as much as he did due to the Mongolian's wolf totem, says Jiang Rong.

It is from wolves that the Mongolians learnt their military tactics. The metaphor goes: the Mongolians are wolves and the Han Chinese are sheep. Wolves follow an extremely ordered social life and survive as a pack; in teams, unlike the sheep; the whole flock of sheep watches with sparkling curiosity when one of their kind is slaughtered, it was probably a way of expressing their relief at not being the one chosen to be killed. Even the tremendous spirits and the ability of the Chinese to build the colossal Wall of China, could not prevent their defeat at the hands of the Mongolians; their sheepishness stood in their way.

Jiang Rong concludes that there is a "binary opposition" between the nomadic and the agrarian culture. Mongols are like indefatigable wolves; in that sense, Mongolia is a spiritual paradise. This is the fundamental message by Jiang Rong in the 700-odd pages of *Wolf Totem*. But in reality, does the spiritual paradise play well in a land of bloodshed, oozing from the jaws of the unrelenting wolves; they kill and devour all life in the grasslands, including humans; and the humans only imitate the wolves.

The part of the novel where the wolves devour young colts is horrific. Such a culture, thriving only on cruelty, violence and bestiality, inspires awe. The wolves' freedom comes at the grand cost of assimilation of other lives. The nomadic chieftain tells Chen Shen that if the wolves did not hunt the gazelles, their population will grow uncontrolled and the grassland will turn into a desert. But wouldn't we all prefer a peaceful desert to a fascist grassland where only one dominating race devours all the others in a macabre ritual of blood.

In Japanese Zen, there is a concept called "*mu*" ; it contains great philosophical truths and can simply be explained thus: A lady being asked, "Your husband who beats you after getting drunk, has he stopped now?" She can neither utter "yes" nor "no"; silence remains the right answer. That is what is explained by the "*mu*" concept of emptiness by Zen. It may have a connection with the void of quantum physics. This may also be an alternative to Jiang Rong's binary opposition.

As I was reading *Wolf Totem*, memories of India's Sufis and seers came to mind. If you call the wolf, a totem, what would you call Adi Sankara, who could make wolves and lions follow him around like puppies?

The most wonderful thing on earth is to give oneself for others. He belonged to the 12th century. He requested his guru to tell him the "*Brahma Rahasyam*". Only after many days of wandering and hunger fasting does the guru tell him the "secret". Once this was completed, the guru warns him, "If you speak of this to others, you will be damned to hell." But the *sishya* climbs the temple tower and yells the secret out loud for the entire village to hear. "If all these people can go to heaven having heard this secret, I don't mind going to hell," he says. He is Ramanuja, the founder of Vaishnavism.

The other wonder is renouncement. For a moment, think on the state of a mind that renounces worldly bonds and wanders in forests, homeless and lonely. Several kings in the history of India may have renounced their all; but nobody compares to Chandra Gupta Maurya, who gave up his all after being India's most powerful emperor. He gave up his throne at the age of forty two, became an ascetic and came to Sravana Belgola. He died in a state of *Sallekhana,* which is a Jain ritual of voluntary death by fasting.

Is there anything more sublime than the ruler of a vast kingdom renouncing all worldly pleasures and leaving this life as an ascetic? Which of the world's totems can explain this?

October 14, 2012

RAPE AND THE INDIAN HOME

The recent gang rape of a 23-year-old girl in the national capital, followed by the death of the victim, has sent shockwaves throughout the country. It has also triggered discussions about the kind of punishments rapists deserve.

There are numerous arguments for and against capital punishment. In my view, our country has not matured enough to bid adieu to capital punishment. Nevertheless, capital punishment by itself will not put an end to these abominable acts. But a faster and sterner enforcement of punishment is sure to help. Few years ago, some college students who had brutally attacked a girl within a cinema complex in Chennai were cleared of all charges with a fine of just a few thousand rupees.

Who fosters this mentality of indulging in violence against women? It is the family and the society. A scene from a recent movie depicts the hero, accompanied by the comedian, waiting at a traffic signal. He asks something to the girl standing beside him. The girl's face is covered. When the girl unveils her face, the hero spits on the road, which is considered as a huge sign of disrespect for the girl, as she is not beautiful. Cinema of no other country can boast of such discriminating scenes. Men who watch and enjoy these films, sexually assault women at the smallest available chance. They catcall schoolgirls, just like the heroes in our films. And if a girl approaches her parents for help, they vitriolize her face. These are not stray incidents; they are reported with a chilling regularity. I used to refer to Delhi as the rape capital when I lived there twenty years ago. Today, the situation has only grown worse rather than improve. Similarly, in Tamil Nadu too, crimes against women are increasing. Those who commit these crimes are usually first-time offenders and the crimes are not predetermined. They are people like us and they live amongst us. They are not strangers or outsiders.

An upper class woman recently said to me that she was sexually abused by a cycle *rickshaw* driver when she was six years old. When I asked her why she hadn't reported him earlier, she said that she was afraid to do so.

There is one other incident that occurred at a Chennai pub. For my friend's birthday, we had a small party; there were four of us - three guys and the girlfriend of a friend. The morning after the party, the girl called me and spoke in a tense voice. She told me that one of our friends at the party had been asking for her number secretively, through gestures that the girl was unable to comprehend. At the end of the party, as they were about to leave, the friend came up to her and said that he was asking for her number. This incident made me think. Is this alright? Or is this the very portrait of a man who may stalk a woman and sexually assault her?

A woman's space is hidebound in our society. She is suffocated inside the family. Nowadays, there is a slight loosening of the boundaries in order to enable women to travel to work. But apart from that, they have no other space outside the family and the workplace.

A few years ago, a girl who had stepped out of a disco was literally chased to death by men who followed her in a car. It happened in Chennai. It happens everywhere. You may recall the moral police who attack women in pubs. The core issue is that women should never move out of their "space". If they do, they will be teased, molested or raped. "What was a woman doing with a man at this hour?" was the question of the offenders in Delhi.

In India, a woman's space is bricked up , trapping her like a jail. If she comes out of her cell, her body is no longer hers. Delhi bags the top spot in this attitude. A slum-dwelling woman who had stepped out early in the morning was kidnapped in a car and gang raped in east Delhi. Last year, in Delhi, a 70-year-old woman was raped by a rickshaw puller and was thrown on a farmland. This incident happened right in front of a police station.

Leave alone Europe and America, countries in the East, do not restrict women's spaces like it is done in India. Recently, when I was in Malaysia, I saw working women everywhere, even at bars, wearing a *tudung* (headscarf), and at men's salons. Remember, Malaysia is an Islamic country. Of course, petty crimes happen — signboards with the warning, "Take care of your footwear", hang everywhere, in temples and pagodas, but crimes against women are unheard of.

The attitude of Indian men towards women is the reason for the increasing number of sexual and other abuse crimes against women in India. A mother plays a significant role in developing her son's views about women. But most men view their mothers and sisters as nothing more than domestic help who wash, cook and assist them. An extension of this view is the common image of treating women as a commodity, meant only for the gratification of men, sexual or otherwise.

Even though we have a culture that worships women as goddesses, crimes against women is rising in number and audacity. Because women have come out of the sacred laws prescribed by men, they are being sexually assaulted and raped — punished for defying "norms". Mahatma Gandhi once said that only if a woman can walk safely on our streets at nights, can we boast of our freedom. If India needs to attain that state of true freedom, our attitude towards women has to witness quite a radical change.

January 3, 2013

HONEY-TRAPPING THE RAUNCHY
NUMBERS

"Hereon there danced youths and maidens whom all would woo, with their hands on one another's wrists... sometimes they would dance deftly in a ring with merry twinkling feet... and sometimes they would go all in line with one another. There was a bard also to sing to them and play his lyre..."

- The Iliad: Book XVIII: Homer

When I worked in Delhi's Civil Supplies Department during the eighties, I was surrounded by Punjabis. I hailed from a rigid and conservative south Indian background, so I was naturally attracted to the Punjabi language and culture. Those wedding dances and festivals, like Holi, dragged me out of my inherent, grim self.

I happened to see a photograph at that time, taken by the German director Ulrike Ottinger during his teens. Through that picture I understood the cultural differences between the northern and southern halves of India. A Tamilian and a Sikh were sitting together in the photo. While the Sikh appeared to be enjoying himself by laughing out loud, the Tamilian's face was simply dingy.

To me it seemed like the Punjabi language carried a musical lilt, probably because of the nasal tones it was spoken in. It was then that I first heard Chamkila and

Amarjot, two legendary Punjabi singers, of whom I became a fan at once. Chamkila's wife Amarjot had a piercing tone which sounded better than Chamkila's. Whenever this pair sang in Punjab, people thronged to hear them —they even climbed lampposts and terraces. On the 8th of March, 1988, Chamkila and Amarjot, along with the members of their band, were shot and killed by militants while they were at Meumpur, Punjab. Chamkila was 28 then. The reason they were assassinated had to do with the content of their songs which celebrated liquor, love and sex. Chamkila sang of extra-marital love, which was intolerable to the extremists. In short, Chamkila was the symbol of the hedonistic lifestyle of the Punjabis.

Dance and music are a part of the Punjabi blood — not as a kind of entertainment, but as the very identity of their existence. While the Tamils from the southernmost part of the country relish dance and music on a hyper-real plane through Tamil movies, the Punjabis involve themselves in the actions and rejoice. In this context, I consider Honey Singh, whose songs wreak havoc amidst the youth of North India, as an extension of the Punjabiyat, idolised by Chamkila and many such singers.

The oppression of dalits, women and other minorities is common knowledge. But the clandestine oppression of students by their parents, educational and social institutions is equally cruel. An apt example would be the statement of the Delhi police commissioner stating that female students must head straight home from college. In a few days, a statement that women must not step out of their homes is imminent. The youth revolt against their adult oppressors through their celebrations, of which Honey Singh is an extreme representative.

I was hooked to Honey Singh as soon after I begun to hear his songs. I must have listened to his *Brown Rang* countless times. It is difficult to capture the ecstatic feel of the song *Chamkila vs Justin Bieber* (written by Honey Singh whose video features Alfaaz), which can always get listeners to shake a leg. This song is a modern rendition of traditional Punjabi folk music, which also serves as a symbol of the Punjabiyat, a symbol of their hedonistic lifestyle.

The youth overcome this societal oppression using their wild imaginations as a weapon. Be it Eminem or Honey Singh — their howls, body language and songs mock society and should be viewed as a metamorphosis of the wild into art: wild aesthetics. For listeners of Indian Classical Music, this observation is out of their league of understanding. Hence, we divide music into two - Thanks to Nietzsche, classical music is the Apollonian type of music while all the Honey Singhs, Gippy Grewals and Alfaazs of the world are classified as the Dionysian.

There have been heavy criticisms against Honey Singh's *Main hoon ek balatkari* and *Ch**** songs. But no one listens to what he has to say about these songs. "I swear on my music, I've neither written nor sung those offensive songs. I'd never dream of singing a song in praise of rape. I completely disown both these obscene numbers. The thought of creating something like that is nauseating to me. I'd rather give up singing than attain popularity through such undignified ways," he said in his defense, and added, "I respect women. What I am going through is another form of rape ... I've sent notices to YouTube and other websites, which display the offensive numbers. I'm a victim of another kind of rape. What's being done to me is among the lowest violations of human dignity." What more is required to prove his innocence? Our anger at violence against women should not be directed at innocents. It is very easy to lay such a trap for anyone through YouTube. The accusations leveled against Honey Singh today were once chucked at Eminem. Even his entry into countries such as Canada and Australia was banned.

The Indian ethos celebrates sex. It is here, on this land, that temples were built for sex and it is here that the formulae for sex were written by our ancestors. The very foundation of the Indian culture is hedonism. Our culture once celebrated and adored sex: the sculptures in our temples stand as timeless witnesses to account for that. In Indian villages, be it at the temple festivals or any other celebrations, dancing and singing remain the fundamental reflectors of our culture that once was. Indian folklore too is known to venerate sex.

The people in villages are less inhibitive about sex than the ones in cities, although in cities most people are desensitized by their consumerist attitudes and consider women to be a sexual commodity. The pelvic movements and gyrations of actors in our movie songs can challenge any pornographic film and yet, their viewer age spectrum begins from a baffling three-year toddler to a nonagenarian. We can grow as sensible human beings only if we move away from this hyper-reality and move into experiencing a life in its real scent, colours and emotions.

Art and Crime are two different things. Hence, it is quite unfair for an artist like Honey Singh to be patronized by society just so it can let off steam for crimes against women.

February 1, 2013

POOR WRITERS, NAKED RAJAS

To me, travelling and reading travelogues remain a bigger passion than writing. Also, reading travel writers like Ibn Battuta is akin to travelling in time. It was my perusal of Battuta, who travelled 75,000 miles over 30 years, that sparked my interest in travel.

In Tamil Nadu, A. Karuppan Chettiar, known as A.K. Chettiar — although not by many — journeyed to several countries in the 1930s to write 17 travel memoirs. He also produced a 50,000 feet long documentary, *Mahatma Gandhi: 20th Century Prophet.* It was a collage of "archival footage" and some of his own filming. Although the abridged version is procurable from American universities, the fate of the original, remains unknown.

The unique feature of Chettiar's travels is that they spanned three decades — form the 1930s to the 1950s — and hence, we get to see two different worlds; one before and one after World War II. A Londoner, who had only just returned from India, once lamented to Chettiar, "I lived peacefully in India. Here, it costs a dog's life for a piece of bread." At a hotel in London where Chettiar stayed, hot water was unavailable. The restaurant was situated on the top floor ; and the kitchen on the ground floor. Orders were shouted downstairs and dishes from the kitchen were pulled up by a rope.

The photographs in his books were another appealing feature of Chettiar's work — they were all shot by Chettiar himself. He studied photography for a year in Japan, in 1935, and once again in 1937, in the U.S. The photographs in the book are all such treasures. But Chettiar's books cannot seem to find a willing publisher. I managed to read his books through photocopies that I borrowed from the private library of R. Krishnamurthy in Pudukottai, Tamil Nadu.

Plenty of Chettiar's voyages were on sea; he took 27 days to reach San Pedro, US, from Japan. Then he journeyed 2,500 miles, from Los Angeles to New York by rail, and travelled through all the northern states by a motor car and once again, arrived in Los Angeles.

There is an interesting paragraph in his book, about his visit to America. He writes:

"Among the Indians who visit New York from India, most of them are *Maharajas*. One *Maharaja* purchased diamonds worth $2,00,000 and forty two cars. At the city centre, there were underground entertainment clubs where the stewardess served in the nude. It was the one place our *Maharajas* visited. During one such visit, one of the *Maharajas* was locked up and was released only after a $5,000 ransom was settled. For what else is a Maharaja blessed with other than wealth?"

While I was applying for a visa at the American embassy, driven by an urge to visit the places that Chettiar had visited, I encountered problems that were experienced by Chettiar too. In those days, "visa on arrival" was the norm. But Chettiar was stopped by the immigration officers when he disembarked at the San Pedro port. Each passenger entering America should possess a minimum of $500, but Chettiar only had $497. After grilling him for over an hour and finally confirming that he was not a Sikh, since America did not easily permit entry of Sikhs into the country even back then, the immigration officer allowed him to enter.

In my case, after all the procedures were over, I stood in front of the immigration officer, answering questions with a smile: "How many children do you have? What does your son do? Are you taking your wife along?" (No, I'm travelling by myself.) "Where will you stay in the US? What do you do?" I replied that I was a writer and showed him a copy of my novel, *Zero Degree*.

After a while he said that my visa could not be sanctioned and sent me on my way. When I asked him for a reason, he handed me a printed paper. Of the three reasons mentioned, I assumed that my visa application could have been rejected for two reasons: first, that I had not convinced the immigration officer that I intended to exit the US, following my temporary stay. Before I had left for the interview, one of my friends had instructed me to tell the officer about my two dogs without fail. Seeing my perplexed expression, he said, "Americans think that you could settle in America even after ditching your wife back here, but it is impossible to part with your dogs. Hence, do not forget to mention them." But since the officer had been interested only in my wife and son, I could not bring up the subject of my dogs — and the fact that my Great Dane, Zorro, will starve and turn into a skeleton until I return. While I apply for my next visa, I should perhaps get some training on how to cleverly steer the conversation towards my dogs.

The second point was to do with finance. I have written on several controversial subjects, but with only a hundred copies of my novel selling, at times, it feels like writing in my personal diary. So you can imagine my financial position. I had to borrow money from my friends, wife and son to travel to the US. Although, I did have some fans there, with whom I could have stayed.

There is only one way to enhance my financial situation: writing for Tamil cinema. But there is a problem — I will have to spend sleepless nights after labeling all those mediocre Tamil films as "classics". Even my greed to follow Chettiar to America will not allow me to ditch my conscience. Perhaps I should write novels with with Lord Rama or Shiva as the protagonists — I could maybe portray them like Akshay Kumar in *Special 26* and sell millions of copies? Does anybody know which IIM coaches you for this? If you do know, kindly help me out.

April 24, 2013

THE WRITER AND THE ALCHEMY
OF DESIRE

Indian Writing in English does not appeal to me because it is either mediocre or boring. Of course there are a few exceptions like G.V. Desani and Irwin Allan Sealy. I read Aravind Adiga's *White Tiger*, which I found interesting but lacking the nuances of a serious work of literature. Hence, I have always had a cautious approach to Indian English fiction. Also, I never dare to touch the writings of those who are popular in a different field. That is the reason I never read Tarun Tejpal's novels, although I am a *Tehelka* fanatic. I have kept with myself, the copies of Tehelka when it used to appear in the tabloids, along with the copies of *Granma* from Cuba, which I subscribed to twenty years ago. Whenever I move, my wife is frustrated with me since these copies travel with me, in the truck. It is against this setting that I happened to read Tejpal's *The Alchemy of Desire,* six months ago.

When Mario Vargas Llosa was awarded the Nobel Prize in Literature, I received more than a hundred messages since I, being the one to have read all his novels twice, was the one who has been promoting his name in Tamil Nadu for the past thirty years. Even though I am a fan of Llosa, he has never influenced my writing. People call me a transgressive writer, but my transgressive comrades like William S. Burroughs, Kathy Acker and Georges Bataille too, have never influenced me because I find them to be boring. But for the first time ever, a book influenced me by a great deal and it was Tejpal's *Alchemy of Desire*. It changed my outlook. Then I read his other two novels. When I finished reading, I thought Tejpal should be placed amongst masters like Fyodor Dostoyevsky and Nikos Kazantzakis.

What I still I don't understand is why Tarun — who has written such extraordinary novels — is known just as a journalist in India. Now, unfortunately, Tejpal has been given the "rapist" title even before his literary contributions can be realized. He is only "accused", but the media seems to have forgotten that the accusations are yet to be proved in court. If proved, he will be punished. If not, can the media take back the colossal damage it has been done to him? I keep wondering if this is how the Indian society wishes to identify a literary genius. The television coverage of this case reminded me of a colony of vultures hovering for a carcass.

At this juncture, a few things come to my mind. The great Chilean poet Pablo Neruda was once a consul in Sri Lanka. At that time, a Tamilian woman — probably a dalit — used to go to his house to clean the latrine. Neruda raped that woman. Remember, he was a communist! Although he did not use the word "rape", that is what he did. He has narrated this incident in his memoirs as follows:

"She walked solemnly toward the latrine, without so much as a side glance at me, not bothering to acknowledge my existence, and vanished with the disgusting receptacle on her head, moving away with the steps of a Goddess. She was so lovely that regardless of her humble job, I couldn't get her off my mind. Like a shy jungle animal she belonged to another kind of existence, a different world. I called to her, but it was no use. After that, I sometimes put a gift in her path, a piece of silk or some fruit. She would go past without hearing or looking. The ignoble routine had been transformed by her dark beauty into the dutiful ceremony of an indifferent queen.

One morning, I decided to go all the way. I got a strong grip on her wrist and stared into her eyes. There was no language I could talk with her. Unsmiling, she let herself be led away, and was soon naked in my bed. Her waist, so very slim, her full hips, the brimming cups of her breasts made her like one of the thousand-year-old sculptures from the south of India. It was the coming together of a man and a statue. She kept her eyes wide open all the while, completely unresponsive. She was right to despise me. The experience was never repeated."

In his *Living in the End Times*, Slovenian philosopher Slavoj Zizek describes the above incident as follows:

"This passage is remarkable not only for obvious reasons: a shameless story of a rape, with the dirty details discreetly passed over ("she let herself be led away, and was soon naked in my bed" — how did she come to be naked? Obviously, she didn't do it herself), the mystification of the victim's passivity into a divine indifference, the lack of elementary decency and shame on the part of the narrator (if he was attracted to the girl, wasn't he embarrassed by the awareness that she was smelling, seeing and dealing with his shit every morning?). Its most remarkable feature is the divinization of the excrement: a sublime goddess appears at the very site where excrements are hidden. One should take this equation very seriously: elevating the exotic Other into an indifferent divinity is strictly equal to treating it like shit."

However, while we read Neruda's poems, this incident does not pop into our minds.

Likewise, Karl Marx had a son, Freddy, born to his maidservant, Helene Demuth. Will Brinda Karat, who is whipping Tejpal now, disown Karl Marx?

In 1997, when he was in the US, Polish film director Roman Polanski was accused of raping a 13-year-old girl. He was convicted, but he fled to France to escape being imprisoned. Since then, he has not returned to the US. Three years ago, he talked about the incident as follows: "I have regretted it for thirty three years." No one identifies him as a rapist. He is recognized as a genius who has created classics like *The Pianist*.

I'm neither justifying the actions of Tarun Tejpal nor am I accusing him. I am a person who believes that it is a crime to even stare at a woman. But one can only be convicted by the law, not by the media.

November 27, 2013

* * *

A RESPONSE WITH REFERENCE
TO THE ABOVE ARTICLE:

I believe that the point I highlighted in my previous article, was misinterpreted. All are equal before the law; literary prowess, wealth or fame are not exempted from it. But before the law takes its course on Tarun Tejpal, the punishment forced upon him, his family and his colleagues, is cruel and even worse than execution. Who will compensate for the disgrace caused to Tejpal's daughter on social networking platforms? What is the answer for the hooliganism portrayed by a politician in front of Shoma Chaudhury's residence?

All I wanted to say is, Hang Shakespeare if he is guilty, but first, know that he is Shakespeare. I only wished to demand where this yarn-spinning media and public were when Tejpal's exciting novels had been published? Novels that were celebrated even outside the borders of India. Why is Tejpal hounded by everybody now, especially by politicians?

In 2001, five murderers were arrested by the Delhi police. It was said that they were a part of the ISI and were sent on a mission to assassinate Tarun Tejpal. Their intention was to kill Tejpal and throw the blame on the BJP, the ruling party back then, as the government was seeking Tejpal's downfall. If the ISI had executed its plan successfully, the BJP government would have lost all its power. Since then, the government had taken a serious interest in protecting Tejpal and gave him a heavy security cover, which lasted nine years. For about six years, there were twenty four armed policemen guarding him around the clock. Wherever he travelled within India, he would be met at the airport by armed officers who escorted him day and night. His house was sandbagged; his office was sandbagged. That eventually became the plot of his novel, *The Story of my Assassins*. No one had portrayed India like Tejpal had in that novel. In fact many were oblivious to the existence of such a writer in India. That is not surprising as we all make a big hue and cry only when someone commits a scandal and becomes infamous.

Tejpal was the one who demonstrated with evidence that India is plagued by corruption, and he put his life on the line for this. If India is witnessing a silent revolution against corruption, it is only because Tejpal was the torch bearer.

Politicians attempt to describe Tejpal as a petty criminal, and by doing so, they want to convey an important message to us , that people like Tejpal – human rights activists, people who fight for justice, those who speak for the marginalized – are all immoral within their personal spaces. Therefore, one should not trust them. It is the politicians who are the right people to take care of us. Thus, I am merely pointing out that the accusation leveled against Tejpal and the happenings sprouting from it, are disproportionate.

The pawns of this game, were cleverly moved.

* * *

THE DEATH OF TASTE

The controversy that erupted in the wake of Tamil writer Perumal Murugan's declaration of his death, his disownment of all his writings, and his request to his readers to burn *all* his novels, not just *Mathorubagan* (One Part Woman), brings with it some very important questions about the freedom of speech and expression in India. We must thank Murugan for two things: one, is obviously for bringing this vital issue of the freedom of speech and expression in India back into the public domain, and two, for unwittingly projecting the spotlight on how Tamil Nadu's particularly vicious brand of politics has made writing nothing more than a mug's game in the state.

Now let us step back a bit. Tamil Nadu's media, the entire Left bandwagon including both political leaders and fellow travellers from the world of arts and books, and Thol Thirumavalavan, the chief of the Viduthalai Chiruthaigal Katchi (VCK), a rabble rousing Dalit politician, were in open solidarity with Murugan and his works.

Despite this massive support, Murugan backed out , asking his publishers to pulp the book and added that he would bear the expenses himself. He asked his readers who had bought his novel to set it on fire, and promised that he would reimburse the money.

History is replete with examples of artistes and creative folk standing up to authority, bigots, bullies, status-quoists and conventional wisdom. But if you want to see creators cravenly surrendering at the very first sight of a controversy, you do not need to look beyond Tamil Nadu and Murugan. The state offers the perfect stage for this farce to play out. The more cynical folk among us could, perhaps, find some of this to be of comic value.

Murugan was summoned by the District Revenue Officer (DRO) to resolve the dispute, thus setting an unhealthy example of dealing with such issues through unofficial channels. It is similar to a traffic cop randomly catching hold of pedestrians and asking them to show him a copy of their tax returns.

Murugan is not the first Tamil writer to be harassed. There are countless others who have been treated like mongrels. H.G. Rasool, a Tamil writer from Nagarcoil, was banished from his community for his writings and not a single soul spoke up for him. When Joe D'Cruz (Sahitya Academy awardee) took a pro-Modi stance during the last parliamentary elections, his English publisher (Navayana) declared that Cruz is into Hindutva and withdrew the translation and publishing project of his novel, *Korkai*. Even now, Cruz is branded as an outcast among his fellow literati. But no one had so much as bothered to offer them a pitiful glance. Murugan must count himself massively lucky to have received such frenzied media attention and the unstinting support of extremely vocal Leftist organizations.

Let us take a look at *Mathorubagan*, the controversial book in question. I picked it up out of sheer curiosity, and was gobsmacked by its amateurish script. It is no different from a potboiler that Kollywood churns out by the truckloads week after week. The story revolves around a woman who is mocked by an entire village for being "barren" and therefore, decides to have an affair out of wedlock for the express purpose of bearing a child, and how this decision of hers led to the suicide of her husband. I know you will run out of fingers to count the number of Indian films which this plot reminded you of.

The story is set a century ago and Murugan says that in that particular village, in Tiruchengode, among women of the Gounder communiy (Murugan mentioned the name of a village and a caste that exists even today), the practice of choosing a male sexual partner out of wedlock at a temple festival to beget a child, was pretty much a way of life. Murugan, however, has not offered any anthropological evidence of this particular practice and when asked to support his distorted imagination with documentary evidence, Murugan claimed his work to be fictitious.

It is not uncommon to have fabricated stories such as these in many parts of the country about women of particular castes, of a particular region. Are these sexually perverted stories true? Extra-marital affairs are common all over the world. But the question here is, does freedom of expression give one the licence to single out women of a particular caste in a village that actually exists without historical proof? Murugan's novel insinuates that virtually all members of the Gounder caste in Tiruchengode have illegitimate ancestry. I view this as a targeted violence on an ethnic group.

This controversy also shows how mediocre writers, with the right political antecedents, are translated, promoted and exported abroad by literary channels that have global influence. Jeyamohan, an A-list Tamil littérateur, hinted at this unholy nexus in his blog recently . However, for some unseemly reason, he decided to remove it soon. This is what he wrote: "This year, *Madhorubagan* might receive many international awards. The reason being that the book's 'English promoters' have already informed the media that it is a critically acclaimed novel. Those (outside of Tamil Nadu) who read the book would nod their heads in agreement with the influential 'critics' and would assume that Perumal Murugan represents the apogee of contemporary Tamil literature. This happens all the time."

While writing this piece, I was invited to a question-answer session with the readers at the Chennai Book Fair. One reader asked if I was right to criticise Murugan when all other writers supported him. I began by saying that I have, for a long time, taken a stand that went against public opinion. "*Madhorubagan* is a mediocre novel which may have found less than average readership in this state where the appetite for literature is pretty weak, but for this controversy. For example, Taslima Nasreen's *Lajja* too, is a mediocre book…" Before I could finish getting my point on *Madhorubagan* across, a representative of the Tamil Nadu Progressive Writers and Artists Association stood up and interrupted me with a scream, "Shut up! It is you who writes trash." he said. I asked, "Don't I have the freedom to pass an opinion on a book? Is it some sort of a holy text?" Regardless, he continued with his barrage of expletives. Pretty soon, he arrived with a few other supporters and tried to physically assault me, threatening to slit my throat. Pandemonium reigned at the venue till they were evicted with help from the police.

The organizers of the book fair and the police requested me to not talk about Murugan as they feared further chaos and trouble. I wanted to spend some more time at the fair, interacting with readers and signing copies of my new novel, but was told to vacate immediately. I was escorted home by men in uniforms.

What an irony it is that Communist supporters who fight for the freedom of Murugan's speech should muzzle mine and try to physically assault me for questioning his work. If this is the fate of free speech and the quality of writers in a state governed by the so-called progressive and rational Dravidian parties, you can only imagine the misery of writers from the former Soviet bloc.

It is scary to say the least.

January 22, 2015

JHUMPA LAHIRI'S "*THE LOWLAND*"

I read Jhumpa Lahiri's *The Lowland* a few days ago. Though the novel refused to grab my attention in the first few pages, it later pulled at me and latched itself to me on the inside. It was one of the few books of world literature which speaks about lovelorn and bereft life; and when I say this, I was reminded of Elfriede Jelinek's *Piano Teacher*. Haunting. Lowland without doubt, left an indelible mark on me.

February 1, 2015

MY SUMMER WISHLIST

Books I wish to read this summer:

* Egyptian journalist and activist, Mona Eltahawy's *Headscarves and Hymens: Why The Middle East Needs A Sexual Revolution.*

I listened to Mona Eltahawy's speech at the JLF 2016. As Elif Shafak, a Turkish author says, it is rare to find a female activist in the Muslim world who can write and talk about sexuality, including her own sexual experiences, so unflinchingly.

* Second on my wishlist is *The Colonel* by Mahmoud Dowlatabadi, doyen of Iranian literature. I have always wanted to read his 3000 page saga of a Kurdish nomadic family, *Kelidar*. It is a ten-volume book that took fifteen years of preparation. Unfortunately, I could not find this book at bookstores. But his other novel *The Colonel* is available in the market. Another reason why I want to read this book is that *The Colonel* was long-listed for the Jan Michalski Prize 2013, along with my novel, *Zero Degree*. And eventually, The Colonel won the prize.

* 'Drawing Blood' by Molly Crabapple because critics say that she could be the Charles Bukowski of our times.

May 8, 2016

THE WRONG COLOUR CODING

In India, the understanding of vernacular literature by the English-speaking elite, is zilch. It is akin to the Western perspective of the East from a few centuries ago. In the modern world, few have a similar opinion about some African tribes. These intellectuals shower their compassion on the regional literati just like those who shower their compassion on the downtrodden. The sympathy of some, particularly that of the English-speaking elite is full of self-reproach and becomes unbearable for those upon whom it is showered. As an example, I could cite the research done in Chennai on dalit literature. Those who take it up are predominantly from the upper castes and hence, they pick up mediocre works that could never qualify as literature, elevate them and brand them as dalit writing. I cannot perceive any difference between "gentlemen" who are amazed to see minimally clothed African tribals and these alleged upper-class dalit researchers.

I could tell that this forms the backdrop of Perumal Murugan's *One Part Woman*. Thanks to the interjection of strange sexual practices in a developed community and the attack on the author by a gang that had no clue about literature, the novel received tremendous popularity. That book is nothing but a normal mainstream potboiler starring Vijayakanth except for the sex-with-stranger-at-a-temple-ceremony part.

Now, Perumal Murugan's *Pyre* stooped to a level lower than any of his previous novels. It laments, in a horrendous way, which is quite similar to the daily scenes we witness outside our places of worship throughout India, how beggars exhibit their purulent scabs and wail for money. The rich who commute in cars, sling awards and amazing reviews stating that they have never come across such a beautiful novel. Shame on us!

In my opinion, *Pyre* is a bad read. It has no literary nuances whatsoever. The incidents and the language used to describe them are unappealing and they resemble the scenes from mainstream films. When the protagonist Kumaresan reaches his village after marrying Saroja, he comes across a middle-aged man and introduces him to Saroja as *Podharu* (which means bush in Tamil used as an insulting reference to the man's hairy body). He adds that if it weren't for the loincloth and the towel he wore, he would have looked exactly like a dark pig: "We call him *Podharu* because that is exactly what he looks like — a bush." Thus, throughout the novel, Kumaresan's neighbouring villagers are treated as a bunch of low lives. Notwithstanding external appearances, the novel portrays these villagers as savages who treat Saroja like an animal because of her fair complexion, just like an actress and because she hails from the city, which indicates a superiority of caste.

The author has conjured his novel based on a lie. In reality, a woman who resembles an actress would be treated like a goddess in a dalit community, not unlike the prevailing Indian attitude of reverence towards anyone with a fair complexion. As a matter of fact, it's dalit men who are tormented and killed by the families of upper-caste girls. Since 2014 till date, 81 people have been killed in the name of "honour". Once, an upper caste politician mentioned love between dalit men and upper class women to be purely cinematic.

But *Pyre* puts up a false front by narrating how an elite, beautiful, fair-skinned girl was burnt to death by ugly, lower caste men. What an anti-dalit regard! Even if the author argues that the men he portrayed were not dalits, the novel clearly delivers the fact that an upper-class woman was harassed and killed by people who were socially inferior to her; whereas in real life, those who suffer are from the lower rungs of society.

Moreover, the idea that a village whose people live in misery, who have been toiling like slaves for centuries together and who are used to genuflection and thrashing, would be so ruthless towards a woman because of her beauty, sounds implausible. In reality, the villagers would have regarded Saroja as a person with power and praised Kumaresan for bringing her to them. Indeed, the reality of Tamil Nadu is that neither would it have been possible for Kumaresan to lead a happy life — if Saroja's kin did not kill him — nor could the loincloth-clad people, who lack arrogance and authority, ever think of setting a woman on fire!

Pyre reminded me of Taslima Nasrin's *Lajja* in many ways, which depicts all Bangladeshis as anti-Hindus who brutally rape Hindu women. *Pyre* too, has a similar hatred as its undercurrent. Literature is love, not hatred.

Since we are bereft of heroes, we keep searching the society's divisions for one — heroes in politics; in social life; among intellectuals; among average men — and Perumal Murugan is a hero to those English-speaking intellectuals who do not have a single clue about the local color!

22 May 2016

HAVE YOU BEEN TO CHENNAI'S
'BOOK UNFAIR'?

The recently concluded book fair held in Chennai was like a music concert held for the deaf. The event, which should have been billed the Book 'Unfair', is usually held in the month of January. But the floods in the city last year forced the fair to be held in June. Such brave decisions seem to have been made by those who don't leave the comforts of their air-conditioned rooms very often. This year it was held in Island Grounds, near the port - where there is not a single tree whose shade you can seek. In the name of beautifying the city, a DMK government cleared out hundreds of trees from this area. In short, the book fair's arena was initially a baking oven.

As the Tamil saying goes, the foot that got hurt shall be the one to receive a fresh blow. At first, the extreme heat kept people away, then it was the torrential rains that prolonged the publishers' pain. Remember old circus tents? The book fair was held in such a tent. Unable to withstand the rain, the tent cloth caved in, leaving the stalls, a watery mess. The book fairs held in Tamil Nadu's other cities such as Madurai, Coimbatore and Erode are much better. At least there, one in ten read literature. Chennai is barren on that count.

I have been to similar events in Thiruvananthapuram

and other cities in India. There, books of the pulp variety get about 10-20% of space. Not more. There are interactive events with authors and publishers on the sidelines. Inside the tent, of the thousand stalls, only fifty hawked literature. Others were dedicated to matters such as making the perfect Manchurian Gobi, how to become a millionaire in a year, hundred varieties of *rangolis*, astrology, yoga etc. The rest was made up of what in Malayalam is called *Paingili* writing, or pulp fiction. No place other than Tamil Nadu considers pulp as literature.

Allow me to lead you back in time, where the roots of this malaise may lie. The Jnanpith Award was first awarded in 1965. The very first one went to Malayalam writing (G Sankara Kurup). Until 1976, no Tamil writer had won the Jnanpith. By then, Kannada, Hindi and Bengali writers had won it twice. In the 40 years since 1976, there has been no improvement. In 1976, Akilan won the award. Then, Jayakanthan in 2002. That is all. Hindi writers have won it nine times; Kannada, eight; Bengali and Malayalam, five each. Malayalam writers who've won Jnanpith include Sankara Kurup, SK Pottekkatt, Thakazhi Sivasankaran Pillai, MT Vasudevan Nair, and ONV Kurup. Similarly, almost every prominent Kannada literary figure (Masti Venkatesha Iyengar, Puttappa, Shivaram Karanth, UR Ananthamurthy, Girish Karnad, Chandrashekhara Kambara) with one or two notable exceptions have received this honour.

The tragedy for Tamil is that the two writers who did win it were both not creators of literature. While Jayakanthan's works weren't outright junk like Akilan's, they were almost exclusively created for popular, large-circulation magazines whose readers preferred comfort reads, not high literature. What K Balachander was to Tamil cinema, Jayakanthan is to writing. Balachander's fans consider him a revolutionary, but he doesn't rank anywhere near world masters. Akilan's writing was untouched by even the shadow of literature. When he won the Jnanpith, Sundara Ramasamy, a giant among Tamil writers, described Akilan's work as a piece of crap writing. He further went on to say, "It is quite natural for the press, and Akilan's fellow entertainers to celebrate his winning of the award. For, when the *jubba* is declared the national attire, pickpockets shall understandably rejoice. One form of mediocrity will naturally embrace and lock its lips with another."

If Modi became the prime minister, I shall leave India, declared the Kannada literary giant U R Ananthamurthy. The statement made waves. It was front-paged by newspapers in Tamil Nadu. Modi won. Ananthamurthy issued a clarification as to why he'll stay put. English dailies in Chennai dutifully reported that too. My question is this: If Ashokamitran had said something similar, nevermind the English papers in Bengaluru, would Chennai dailies have written about it? They would not have because here, no one even knows the names of Tamil litterateurs.

Who will recommend their names for the Jnanpith? How will those seated at Delhi know about them if no one even spoke of them here? In Tamil, there is no dearth of writers worthy of such high honour. To name a few, we have Indira Parthasarathy, Na. Muthusamy, Sa. Kandasamy, Gnanakoothan, Ashokamitran, and A. Madhavan. These are writers who are still plying their trade. Before them were giants such as Thi. Janakiraman, M.V. Venkatram, S. Sampath, Thanjai Prakash, Ku.Pa. Rajagopalan, La.Sa. Ramamrutham, C.S. Chellappa, Ka.Naa. Subramaniam, Na. Pichamurthy, and possibly twenty five others who could and should have bagged awards such as Jnanpith. There was no one to tell the Delhi-decision making panel about their literary prowess because no one knew of their existence, and/or no one cared.

I spotted the mighty Gnanakoothan at one of the book fair stalls this year. Hardly anyone present could even recognize him. That was because no one had even heard of him. There was something more tragi-comic. Manushya Puthiran is one of the most prominent poets in Tamil. He's also a publisher, and a leading face on television, weighing in on social and political matters almost every day. He was sitting outside the stall put up by his publishing house. A common man who watched him only on the telly, asked him with a quizzical look, 'What on earth are you doing here at the book fair, sir?'

Let me recount another incident that took place a few days earlier. I was speaking to a friend inside the sweaty circus tent when people suddenly fled to the exit as if there was a fire or an earthquake. Then, some fifty men materialized from nowhere, shoving people aside, asking them to clear out. When I tried to make sense of the melee, I saw the beaming face of celebrity film lyricist Vairamuthu.

There was a posse of hundred people stalking him. There was a mini riot. For a minute, my friend thought the organizers had brought the joys of *jallikattu* to the book fair.

At no literary festival in the world would you encounter a more vulgar sight. Vairamuthu is a good lyricist. In the Mani Ratnam film '*Ayutha Ezhuthu*' he had penned a lovely song employing pair words. But like many others in Tamil Nadu, the disease of portraying oneself as a literary figure of great importance afflicts him too. You cannot blame him because a collection of his short stories sold in lakhs, and within one year of launch, the publisher had to issue ten reprints of the book. Now Vairamuthu goes around asking unsuspecting members of the general public why he shouldn't be given the Nobel. I can assure you; this happens only in Tamil Nadu.

PS: A few days ago, my local butcher, upon seeing me walk past his shop, waved at me and said: 'Hello, Vijay TV *saar*.' As it happened, I was a guest on one of Vijay TV's largely popular talk shows, that week. After that incident, I'd decided not to show my face on TV.

June 13, 2016

GNANAKOOTHAN: THE GREATEST TAMIL POET SINCE SUBRAMANYA BHARATI.

(The pioneer of modern Tamil poetry, R Ranganathan, better known by his pen name, Gnanakoothan died on 28 July, 2016. Having been born in a Kannada household, Gnanakoothan was the most important Tamil poet post-Subramanya Bharati.)

On the 23rd of July, at around 8 p.m., I felt this sudden urge to visit Gnanakoothan. Only a few days ago I had sought his help to decode a Sanskrit poem. When I rang him up to make an appointment, he told me that he would come down to meet me himself.

Gnanakoothan was too modest for his own good. It was one of the major reasons as to why he did not get the kind of attention and recognition from the Tamil society which a man of his accomplishment and skill deserved. After all, when cinema had turned Tamil Nadu into an inferno, how can the tender voice of a poet remain audible? Here, if you don't blow your trumpet loud enough to shatter people's eardrums, they would scarcely notice a writer's existence.

The day I wanted to meet with Gnanakoothan, he had bid adieu to the world of poetry.

When I heard the news of his demise, I was shattered. I couldn't muster the will to pay my last respects.

But Gnanakoothan is immortal. He represents the link between the glorious and ancient Sangam Tamil literature and the twenty first century. The Sangam poets celebrated their Land in their songs. Land meant the life it sprouted, its Gods, its smells and sounds, animals, stories, chastity; its sorrows; joys and jollities.

The French New Wave dragged cinema, kicking and screaming, into the real world of common folk from other-worldly epics and stories of kings and queens. Similarly, Gnanakoothan brought Tamil poetry that was floating somewhere in the realms of high philosophy back to *terra firma* inhabited by ordinary men and women. In that sense, he can be called the pioneer of modern Tamil poetry.

Just as how after several centuries Tamil received a new lease of life at the hands of Subramanya Bharati, Gnanakoothan was singularly responsible for bringing about the next turning point in Tamil Literature. He was a scholar of both Sanskrit and Tamil literature. He had read Bhasa's and Kalidasa's originals in Sanskrit. At the same time, his mastery over Western literature was immense. His works were enriched by a deep understanding of these three different literary traditions.

Gnanakoothan was the most affable, mild-mannered person you could meet. But his poetry was uniformly provocative and incendiary. Most notably, by employing biting satire and parody, he attacked the Dravidian movement which according to his opinion, used a counterfeit brand of Tamil pride to further its political ambition.

Sample these two verses which he wrote to counter the Tamil chauvinists during the pinnacle of the language movement:

Every language is a gem

Cut away the anger my friend

Tamil is one of them

* * *

Tamil is my life breath too

But I won't puff it onto you

The Dravidian parties rode to power on the back of Tamil nationalism, but during their reign, Tamil began to lose ground. You could finish a graduate course in this state without having to learn a single word of Tamil. Gnanakoothan lampooned all of this back in the 1970s.

Another important feature of his oeuvre was iconoclasm. There were no holy cows for him. Take for instance, this poem on Lord Nataraja:

O King of dance!

Dance your reckless jig

In your whirl let all directions rattle and roil

But ensure no harm to my bottle of oil

Until you break it

you have a place at my table

It is astonishing that this trailblazer of modern Tamil verse hadn't been given the Sahitya Akademi award. But for the Vishnupuram prize awarded by the Tamil writer Jeyamohan's foundation last year, Gnanakoothan would not have a single literary award gracing his cabinet.

The legendary Bengali writer Mahasweta Devi died the same day as Gnanakoothan. The English dailies in Chennai recorded her demise on Page One, while the news of Gnanakoothan's death was buried deep within the pages.

Of Tamil's many miseries, Gnanakoothan's unheralded literary life, ranks pretty high.

July 30, 2016

AUTHORS DO NOT EXIST IN TAMIL NADU

The words 'writer' or 'author' can conjure many images in your minds. However, I can tell you with a fair degree of certainty that none of them would make sense in the context of Tamil Nadu or Tamil Writing because there are no writers in Tamil Nadu.

How then would we account for hundreds of Tamil writers churning out world class novels, short stories and poetry? This could be the subject of study of multiple PhD theses. In the West too, there is a long list of writers and artistes who lived in penury, on the margins of mainstream society. Think of Arthur Rimbaud, Franz Kafka, Kathy Acker, Charles Bukowski.

But there is one fundamental difference between them and Tamil writers. Bukowski spent many years of his life in the company of trash cans, but during his own lifetime, he was acknowledged as a veritable icon in the United States. In Tamil Nadu, not more than five hundred people would know of writers such as Si. Su. Chellappa, Ka.Naa. Subramaniam, M.V. Venkatram, S. Sampath, Nakulan or Thanjai Prakash who sacrificed their lives for literature. Their brilliant work gushed out like a jungle cascade, that remained unseen, unmarvelled, unremarked. Tamil lives on, thanks to the sacrifices of such creators.

Chellappa sold his property and personal possessions to run a literary magazine called *Ezhuthu* in the 1960s. It was this magazine that introduced a whole new generation of modern Tamil litterateurs to the world. Ashokamitran can hold a place among the greatest writers of the world. There are at least a dozen writers in Tamil deserving of the Nobel, who have practiced the craft for nearly half a century. I would be surprised if even a thousand people in the state know their names. The older generation reconciled with this situation proclaiming it destiny. The younger generation's response is self-destruction.

I addressed students of a university which is more than a hundred-years-old and has produced two Nobel laureates. The university's vice-chancellor had not heard of me despite being associated with the Tamil department. More disconcertingly, he walked up to me and said, "I vaguely remember seeing you on TV."

At such times, imagine the health of younger writers who have to transform their lives and souls into the wax and wick that keeps the flame of Bharati, Chellappa and Ka.Naa. Subramaniam alive. Many young poets drink themselves to death. It is not uncommon to see Tamil writers as young as thirty five losing the battle against alcoholism. A few years ago, I spent five days with the young poet Kumara Gurubaran at the Jaipur Litfest. Not a day passed where he wouldn't tell me that he was my son. He would drink all night and sleep through the day. I told him, "Kumara, often I too have felt like starting my day with a glass of whisky. Why even spend my entire day in the company of cocktails? I don't do it because I'd die."

His response was, "What do we gain by merely being alive, Charu?"

Besides the lack of identity and recognition, the other major problem for Tamil writers is the absence of a sustainable income. I have made no money in my forty-year-long writing career. There is no question of being paid by small literary magazines that publish my pieces. Widely circulating commercial magazines pay a rupee a word, with the maximum limit being Rs 750. There is no money to be made in television either. News channels believe they do writers a favour by having them on air.

The lot of film writers pretty much find themselves in similar situations. Now, films are made on multi-million dollar budgets. The actors, directors and music composers earn in crores. Dialogue, screenplay, and song writers are paid a lakh or two, if they are in luck, and when the cheques do not don't bounce. According to media reports, there were dishonoured cheques worth several lakh rupees in the possession of Na. Muthukumar , the high-profile lyric writer who died a few weeks ago. There is no bigger name than Vairamuthu when it comes to lyric-writing in the Tamil filmdom. He is the recipient of multiple National Awards. There is not a nook in the state where his songs cannot be heard. He too sails in the same boat as far as financial rewards go. Why? The harsh reality is that even if you wield your pen like Vairamuthu does, no one would want to pay you.

Recently, one marquee director decided to pay a well known writer to pen dialogues for his film, not in cash, but in ten bottles of French brandy costing roughly seven thousand rupees a pop. What the directors are indirectly hinting at is that writers get the privilege of being associated with celebrities so popular that they should not have worry about getting paid. Those associated with films at least get a share of the spotlight. In the world of publishing, even that is non-existent. How many people would have heard about A-list Tamil poets such as Devadachchan and Devadevan. Probably even their family members do not know about their prowess.

There lived a writer called Pa. Singaram (1920 - 1997). Every single Tamil writer would rank his novel *Puyalile Oru Thoni* (A boat in the storm) as the best novel ever written in Tamil. Singaram could not find anyone to publish the novel. Therefore, he did not write any other. For nearly forty years he was a nondescript employee working for the *Daily Thanthi* newspaper. No one knew he was a writer. Is this not another form of suicide?

Almost every interview with Ashokamitran offers a peek at the bitter and shameful life that Tamil writers have to endure. What is even more shameful is that common folk casually throw accuses at young writers who die of being drunks and wastrels.

A cat called Chintoo lives in my house. Every day, he wakes up in the morning, eats, plays, and sleeps; gets up in the afternoon, eats some more, plays some more and sleeps some more. A cat can do that. Can humans live like cats? Such unthinking men who lead such an existence, have the cheek to ask artistes not to drink!

August 27, 2016

ASHOKAMITRAN (1931-2017): A GENIUS BOTTLED IN OBSCURITY WHO DESERVED FAR, FAR MORE.

It is hard for me to write about Ashokamitran without being hit by a torrent of emotion. I regard him as not only my guru but my father, who brought me into this world, sustained me and nourished me. Ours was like most father-son relationships. The *rasa* of my writing is entirely borrowed from him. He is my progenitor. But he could never warm up to my writing. And knowing that, I stayed away from him.

In 1968-'69, Ashokamitran's novel *Karaindha Nizhalgal* (Dissolved Shadows) was serialized in a magazine called *Deepam.* It formed the foundation of my writing, though I was too young to realise it at the time. Over the next three decades, I read every word Ashokamitran wrote. While working in Delhi, I would constantly carry with me, a copy of his short story collection, *Kaalamum Aindhu Kuzhandhaigalum* (Time and the Five Children) like it was a talisman.

Ashokamitran was the managing editor of the Tamil literary magazine *Kanaiyazhi* from 1966-'89. The letters to the editor that I sent regularly, published under the name "Nivedita from Delhi" marked my entry into the world of writing. Subsequently, the magazine published my first short story, *Mull* (Thorn). Ashokamitran wrote me a postcard, appreciating my contribution. Whenever I was in Chennai, I would make it a point to pay him a visit at his home located in a quiet lane opposite the T Nagar bus stand.

That was in the 1980s. When I met him a decade later, the house had turned into an apartment block. Writing was his only source of income. The English magazines would pay him pittance and Tamil publications were even worse. His new apartment had lost the beauty and tranquility of his former house.

In 1999, I approached Ashokamitran with the request to write a foreword for my short story collection, *Nano*, which included some stories he had published in *Kanaiyazhi*. He did write the foreword – as was his wont, on the backside of an advertisement flyer because he often did not have the money to even afford basic stationary – but in it, he said he disapproved of much of my writing. Metafiction was not the genre for him, he wrote. After that, our contact was minimal but my devotion to his writing that began at the age of fifteen, remained intact. In fact, it has only increased with each passing day.

In the late '80s, when I re-read Ashokamitran after having immersed myself in World literature, a question arose in my mind for which I am yet to find an answer. People pray to god seeking fulfilment of many desires. My only prayer is to find this answer.

It needs a bit of explaining. I recently read Orhan Pamuk's *Istanbul*, translated into Tamil by G. Kuppuswamy.

Pamuk writes in great detail about another Turkish literary giant, Ahmet Hamdi Tanpinar. Interestingly, Tanpinar's works have been translated into Tamil, and possibly, other Indian languages as well. Similarly, almost every important European writer has been translated, discussed and debated in Tamil.

I would argue that Ashokamitran is a greater writer than Kafka or Camus. In the Indian subcontinent, I would rate him higher than even the great Saadat Hasan Manto. Why, then, is he not studied in any great detail abroad or even in Indian universities? Why is he not as famous in the Czech Republic as Milan Kundera is in Tamil Nadu?

It is easier to understand Ashokamitran's lack of popular acclaim in his homeland, Tamil Nadu, where only those who write for the state's Kollywood film industry matter. But Ashokamitran is one of the very few Tamil writers whose work has found exceptionally good English translators. Even then, obscurity is what he had to live with. The largest selling English daily in Ashokamitran's hometown, Chennai, carried a 500 word report on his death on Thursday on the inside pages. Why does it have to be so? That is the question I ask.

Imagine a literary colossus like Ashokamitran moving around the streets of Chennai in a rickety old bicycle. That was his lot. He gave up the cycle during the very last years of his life, when he had become too weak. When a fellow Tamil writer, during an interview, asked him about his frail health, Ashokamitran said it was because he would often not have the means to eat well in his youth.

A mere listing of the titles of Ashokamitran's books over a 60-year career could constitute a 1,500-word essay. Each one is a piece of glowing ember. There is not one book that could be termed ordinary. *Ottran* (The Spy), *Pathinettavadhu Atchakkodu* (The Eighteenth Parallel), *Thanneer* (Water) and *Inspector Shenbagaraman* are classics. *Karaindha Nizhalgal* is a short novel but it took me a good ten days to finish upon re-reading it recently. The tragedy and the farcical lives of Ashokamitran's characters can bring readers to tears.

Ashokamitran's decade-long stint at Chennai's Gemini film studios served as the raw material for *Karaindha Nizhalgal*. But this is a novel about the film industry. It is about people. Natarajan and Rajagopal, the production managers, Natarajan's assistant Sampath, Producer Reddy, studio owner Ram Iyengar, his son Pachha, the actress Jayachandrika, desperate-for-a-film role Velu and Shanmugam – all their stories could rival the character arc of a Greek tragedy.

The effusion of empathy in Ashokamitran's novels was a result of his honesty. He maintained that he was merely paying a tribute to the men and women he met in real life through the characters in his stories. There was no effort to forcibly squeeze out the drama where none existed. Ashokamitran said he wrote *Karaindha Nizhalgal* sitting on a cement bench in T. Nagar's Natesan Park. That bench should be a place of worship for any lover of literature. At every literary event I attend, I unfailingly urge people to read each one of his works. It is a privilege to have lived in the same era as a writer of Ashokamitran's brilliance.

With his eye for detail in capturing the humdrum reality, a ear for dialects, the precision and economy of language and a naturalist view that looked at humanity bottled in by powers beyond its control, Ashokamitran, some say, was Charles Dickens, Anton Chekov and Emile Zola rolled into one. But, he was much more than that.

March 24, 2017

ASHOKAMITRAN

Ashokamitran's body was nothing but bones covered with skin. He had a forlorn look on his face but was a joy to talk to and was a man with an amazing sense of humour. He would rarely laugh but his jokes were deep and perspicacious and his humour mostly dark.

During one of my frequent meetings with him over the past year, he once passingly mentioned that he weighed only 45kgs. That bony body was cremated at the Besant Nagar electric crematorium at a funeral that was witnessed by two dozen people - mostly long-time friends.

The Karnataka Government declared a holiday when Kannada writer U. R. Ananthamurthy died three years ago and the declared mourning period was a week long. But sadly, the death of Ashokamitran has not sparked a single wave of shock in Tamil society which often celebrates mediocrity. Ashokamitran is undoubtedly Tamil literature's greatest asset. The way he portrayed women in his works has perhaps not even been achieved by women writers of his time. His story `Vizhaa Maalai Pozhudhu' (The Festive Evening) revolves around a teenager from Andhra Pradesh who wants to become a Kollywood actress. The part where the sixteen-year-old cries, pouring her heart out before a deity over her pitiful plight in the pursuit of films, still lingers fresh in my mind like a painting. The story `*Iruvar*` (Two People) deals with a young widow who returns to her maternal house only to be mercilessly beaten up by her brother for talking to her husband's mistress when she was made to sit outside during her period. She dies of a high temperature. Ashokamitran has penned hundreds of such female characters.

His stories are simple, easily comprehensible to a common reader, yet contain deep philosophical visions. In his story `*Eli*` (The Rat) written four decades ago, he describes a middleclass house with the metaphor of a small rat burrow. In the story, Ganesan, his wife, his sister and his daughter have to sleep in the same room and the tiny house is haunted by a bunch of rats. The rat trap needs a piece of solid food like dosa or vada. But sadly, only semi-solid food like upma and pongal are cooked in the poor household. Any other dish is a luxury. It is 10 p.m. when Ganesan finally decides to buy a vada for the trap. The restaurants are closed. A public meeting is happening where the speaker is warning Nixon, Britain, Russia, Pakistan and Indira Gandhi, and the leaders of Tamil Nadu. The narrator comments that the intensity of the warnings was so strong that if they had reached the ears of the rat family, they would have jumped into the Bay of Bengal themselves. Finally, one day a rat gets trapped and Ganesan frees it into the open. But the rat is unaccustomed to open spaces and it topples and struggles, only to be picked up by a crow. Ganesan feels guilty and sorrowful about the rat's plight. He is also bothered that the vada he had put in the rat trap remained without being consumed.

In the novel `*Karaindha Nizhalgal*`, the protagonist Natarajan, a production manager with a film company, starves for three days without food and ends up vomiting after eating a vada. I wonder about the number of days where Ashokamitran had to suffer the brunt of hunger so that he could support his family with the meagre income of a professional writer. He had to provide for the education of his three sons. But never did I see him exhibit self-pity. The palatial house of a famous personality stood opposite his son's house and when I asked him about it, he said something which I will never forget: "A writer is one who has no source for his next meal". This is the philosophy of saints and wise men in India.

Through his meditative eyes and sparkling pen, we learned a lot about the human condition.

March 27, 2017

POLITICS

NO JOKES ON THE PALM LEAF

Back in Delhi, I am told, Mani Shankar Aiyar is famous for his witty ripostes, sharp one-liners and punch lines that have audiences in splits. So I set out for Mayiladuthurai, expecting to be vastly entertained, only to find that in his constituency, the venerable Congress candidate cuts a very different figure. The starched white kurta-pyjama that the cabinet minister wears in Delhi has been replaced by the local garb of dhoti and shirt.

And it has been a long time since Aiyar made a joke here, at least in public. That last joke was in 2003, when Jayalalitha, on the advice of her astrologers, gifted an elephant to the Guruvayur temple in Kerala. Aiyar found the image that this conjured up, irresistible. He remarked, no doubt in an allusion to the *Puratchi Thalaivi*'s elephantine proportions, that she could just as well have gifted herself to the temple. Alas, the queen was not amused, nor were her loyal supporters. Just a few days later, Aiyar was waylaid and attacked by AIADMK men near Nagapattinam, slippers were thrown at him in his own constituency, and his office was ransacked.

That incident taught him a salutary lesson about the perils of shooting his mouth off. But another reason why Aiyar is uncharacteristically solemn and sober in his speeches in Mayiladuthurai is, quite simply, that his Tamil is not fluent enough for him to pun or play on words. In fact, to the locals, Aiyar's Tamil, is in itself something of a joke—they describe it as a bizarre mix of Brahmin Tamil and the halting Tamil spoken by foreigners. "It reminds us of Subramanian Swami," people in Mayiladuthurai tell me. "He's another one who speaks this kind of strange Tamil." Another thing the locals find strange, is that Aiyar affixes his caste to his name. "Which politician in Tamil Nadu does that, especially if you have a Brahmin surname!" they say incredulously.

Mani Shankar Aiyar's mantra, ever since he first contested from Mayiladuthurai in 1991, has been: "I shall make Mayiladuthurai the Dubai of India!" Some may wonder why on earth Mayiladuthurai, a bastion of Tamil culture, would ever want to be Dubai. In this constituency stands the magnificent 12th century Chola temple of Darasuram in Kumbakonam. The ancient port city of Poompuhar, home of Kovalan and Kannagi, the protagonists of the great Tamil epic *Silappadikaram* , is here too. Mayooram Vedanayagam Pillai, author of the first Tamil novel, *Prathaba Mudaliyar Chariththiram*, written in 1857, hailed from here—he was the village munsif. Literacy and education levels have been high here for a long time.

No, Aiyar has not quite brought glittering Dubai-style shopping malls to Mayiladuthurai. But there is no denying that he has brought development to his constituency. The roads here are of a smoothness to rival Hema Malini's cheeks. The villages look prosperous and clean, with drinking water, electricity, toilets, community centres and even well-tended graveyards. I am shocked when I enter the toilet at the city bus stop. "I have to pay two rupees to take a leak here?" I ask incredulously. The man at the toilet door apologises: "I feel horrible having to do this." Must be a Dubai custom, imported to Mayiladuthurai.

Among Aiyar's other gifts to Mayiladuthurai are a gas plant, a thermal power plant, and yet another power plant fuelled by sugarcane waste. There is also an impressive Rs20-crore stadium, better than any in Chennai, much used by local students. But there are not enough employment opportunities for the local population. Many go abroad to seek their fortunes. "This brain drain is one of the reasons why this place hasn't yet become Dubai," Aiyar tells me, looking rather dejected. His characteristic ebullience is definitely missing. And with reason.

His opponent, O.S. Manian of the AIADMK, is a well-networked local man, who people say, participates closely in their daily lives and problems. Manian emphatically points out that when more than 90 children died in a fire at a school in Kumbakonam, he was right there to help and console, whereas Aiyar, was unable to reach immediately. "When we local people approach Aiyar with a problem, he pushes us away, saying such local matters don't come under an MP's purview," complains Manikandan, who runs a small stall at the Mayiladuthurai town bus stop. Many others echo similar views.

But what seems to have made this election battle a really uphill one for Aiyar is the wave of public sentiment against Karunanidhi, whose DMK is the Congress party's alliance partner in Tamil Nadu. Karunanidhi's five-hour after-breakfast to pre-lunch "fast", with his first wife sitting at his feet and his second wife at his head—a scene aired repeatedly on Sun TV and Kalaignar TV—has earned him widespread ridicule. Aiyar has also been hit by the Congress's own stand on the Tamil Eelam issue—it is seen to be looking the other way while thousands of Eelam Tamils face death and disaster. After Rajiv Gandhi's assassination by the LTTE, local Tamils had distanced themselves from the Eelam cause. But that was 19 years ago, and now it is again an emotive issue for them. "So many Tamils are being killed by the Eelam—what's Aiyar doing about that?" a municipal sweeper asks me heatedly.

Jayalalitha, meanwhile, has done an about-turn. "Support our alliance and I shall fight for a separate Eelam till my death" is her new trumpet call. Her election rallies show her at her histrionic best. Referring to the DMK taunt that she knows nothing about children or family, she turns to the crowd, arms outstretched, and pleads, "Aren't you my family? Aren't you my children?" The crowd roars back, "Yes! Yes!"

A popular AIADMK slogan in Mayiladuthurai these days, mockingly asks: *"arukku naadi paarkalaama"* "what do the palm leaves say about Aiyar?" The palm leaves refer to Mayiladuthurai's famous Vaitheeswaran Kovil, well-known for its centuries-old palm leaves with astrological predictions written on them. You go there, give your name, and you will be shown a palm leaf on which your destiny is written. Even if your name is Obama, you will find your palm leaf, I am told.

As I wait near a bus stop, baking in the sun and while the photographer goes in search of the shots he wants, three women approach me. They are middle-aged, heavily caked with powder and paint. "You want to come?" they ask. "Forget about my coming," I answer, "what do you think of the coming election?" "First attend to us, then we'll tell you about the election," they laugh. Unfortunately, at that moment, the photographer comes back and hurries me off to our meeting with Mani Shankar Aiyar.

"Write this in bold letters," Aiyar instructs me, as his parting shot: "Dubai is collapsing, but Mayiladuthurai is growing rapidly." I do not ask him if he has consulted the palm leaves.

May 18, 2009

MODERN OUTLOOK STILL ELUDES US

Chennai stands first in the whole of India when it comes to moral policing. The reason? The semi urban, semi-feudal Tamil society is still not ready to accept modern thoughts. Chennai cannot be called a cosmopolitan city just by looking at the huge malls and multiplexes. This is one city in India where foreigners are seldom seen.

A few years ago, the police manhandled couples sitting in the Anna Nagar park. They were dragged to the police station, their parents were called in and warned, and the boys sent to Vellore prison. The police commissioner issued a general apology a few days later. In spite of this, Chennai's approach towards moral policing has not changed.

Recently, the Chennai police bought a few bikes that can be driven on sand. You might have guessed the reason by now. The bikes are to be used as a means of surveillance, to keenly watch couples sitting on the beach. This is the first time in India where any state has done anything like this.

Apart from the Chennai police, political parties, media and religious institutions are also resorting to the moral high ground on this issue. Magazines and papers publish pictures of women, taken during cocktail parties or when they are sitting on the beach. Is this not an offence under law? Does this not amount to trespassing into an individual's life? But importance to the individual's rights is not given in India. We cannot even think about this kind of an invasion of privacy in developed countries. The existing laws in India were formed during the British rule and are still practiced. Even in Britain, these laws have been long discarded.

Political parties are not any different. A few years ago, when a Jain monk, well over 70 years old, tried to enter Tamil Nadu, he was humiliated by the Dravida Kazhagam and RSS activists because he was naked. Jain saints, who are naked throughout their lives, are forced to hide their private parts inside Tamil Nadu. Opposing the saint were two political outfits with opposite agendas — one declares there is no god while the other believes in god.

Nothing can be done, out in the open, in Tamil Nadu. Only in privacy. If an adult male and female want to spend time together, they cannot do so. Since the society and the state are hypocritical, there is no private space for the common man. They cannot go to restaurants, they cannot go to public places like the beach. A few weeks ago, there was a raid at some pubs in Chennai. A number of youth were arrested. The boys were put in lockup and the girls, sent home with a warning. Their crime? They were drinking at night in pubs. Since the government is conservative and moralistic, the police too, behave likewise.

Recently, a PhD student from the University of Madras was talking with a male friend at the Indira Nagar MRTS station, and a police inspector felt the need to object to it.

The inspector threatened the woman and said he would call her husband. Even after she told him that the man was a friend of her husband's, he continued to ill-treat them. The couple was saved when the public interfered.

Who will educate the police? The government generates power. It is its duty to educate. But if the government itself is not progressive in its outlook, who will educate the police? It is high time the intelligentsia and media started doing something about it.

December 31, 2010

CAMP AS CULTURE

The cocktail of Kollywood and Dravidian politics has ensured Tamil Nadu remains an intellectual backwater. Twenty years back, when people asked me about my profession, I would tell them I was a writer. They demanded to know the police station I was posted at. It was not just my close-cropped hair and big moustache that convinced them I was a policeman. The police force too, employs people designated as 'writers'. Their job is to write out complaints and FIRs. Today when I introduce myself as a writer, the follow up question is inevitably about the film scripts I have worked on.

I am sure you can make out that a writer does not have an identity in the Tamil society. The provocative French philosopher, Jacques Lacan coined the phrase *la femme n'existe pasabout.* The non-existence of the sexual identity of a woman. In the context of Tamil Nadu, I can paraphrase Lacan to say *l'ecrivain n'existe pas* or that *the writer has no identity.*

Modern Tamil literature's golden era spanned from the 1930s to1970s. Writer and journalist Ku.Pa. Rajagopalan (pen name Ku Pa Ra) formed the Shakespeare Club in Kumbakonam in 1921 where every week, writers met and discussed world literature. Works of writers such as Kalki (best known for historical novels such as '*Ponniyin Selvan*') and Devan, a humour writer, were extremely popular among women back then. But today Tamil has shrunk to being just a spoken language. The written word is off-limits for most young people because they simply cannot read the Tamil script.

Tamils have lost their reading habit. As a society, we have become 'mega-serial' television addicts. I am considered to be a popular writer in the state. However, my fellow authors and I need nothing short of a miracle to sell even a 1,000 copies. To put this in perspective, in China, Jiang Rong's '*Wolf Totem*' has sold nearly thirty million copies. Why, even in neighbouring Karnataka, S.L. Bhyrappa's new releases are eagerly awaited and copies fly off the shelves at such a pace that publishers have to go in for reprints with a week of launch.

This cultural debasement started when the Dravida Munnetra Kazhagam (DMK) came to power in 1967, eighteen years after the party was formed, thanks to their anti-Hindi agitations of 1965. That year, the DMK declared Republic Day as a Black Day. Congress was accused as anti –Tamil because of its pro-Hindi image, and people revolted against the Congress; the violence that ensued was uncontrollable. Nearly 70 people died. A few students set themselves on fire. That was the start of a vicious tradition which continues even today. When a politician loses an election or gets imprisoned, there are always some diehards ready for fire sacrifice.

The irony here is that the DMK whose calling card was

linguistic chauvinism, that provoked people against Hindi, made Tamils turn away from their own mother tongue. I can think of two reasons why they succeeded. Fed by a steady diet of ethnic and cultural supremacy, the Tamils were bewitched by the tales spun by self-serving politicians. There was no language sweeter than Tamil, and no culture more ancient and glorious than that of the Tamils'.

In 1968, the World Tamil Conference convened by the then Chief Minister C.N. Annadurai, attracted millions. It felt like Allahabad's Kumbh Mela. M.Karunanidhi who succeeded Annadurai, erected scores of statues of Sangam era poets and personalities to celebrate the hoary Tamil civilization. The most notable among those was the statue of Kannagi on Chennai's Marina beach, who was the lead character in 'Silapathikaram', one of the five great epics in Tamil, penned in second century AD.

Chief Minister Karunanidhi was likened to the Chola kings and he lapped up every bit of such praise that came his way. Chola kings who conquered many Asian countries were honored in a grand ceremony. Wherever Karunanidhi went, there was a coronation of sorts. It became customary for Karunanidhi to be offered a crown of flowers – of course, India being a democratic country, we were spared the sight of him being crowned with a real one.

But this cultural degradation cannot be blamed on Karunanidhi or politicians of his ilk alone. It was a two-way street. The society had unquestioningly bought into the story of Tamil cultural exceptionalism. Dravidian leaders and their subjects praised and patted each other on the back so often that a bemused writer those days exclaimed, "Yes! The first ape was also a Tamil!"

While the DMK kept itself in power, stoking ethnic pride and manufacturing tales of Tamil glory, Tamil as a language faced relegation. It began disappearing from private English medium schools and DMK's policies ensured that a student could finish schooling without as much as a basic proficiency in Tamil. Tamil Nadu's education system produced youngsters who had proficiency in neither English nor Tamil.

A Tamil film's audio release function that I attended recently, commenced with the recital of the Tamil Anthem (is there a place in the world where a language is worshipped in the form of a song?). We dutifully stood up in attention. The film's producer, director, music director, and most of the crew was Tamil, but spoke a variant of their mother tongue that was remarkably Anglicized. I think it is customary for the Tamils to pulverize their own culture first, then hold it up as something sacred and offer ritual genuflections. Being a writer in this society, as I often lament, is like being a painter in a country of the blind, or a musician among the tone deaf. I feel like a goldsmith in a country of beggars.

The DMK's role in making Tamil Nadu an intellectual backwater does not end there. After the DMK came to power, the Tamil Brahmins began moving to north India first, and then to North America, piggybacking on the software boom. Hostility towards the Brahmins was virtually institutionalized. EV Ramaswamy or 'Periyar', the leader of the Dravidian movement instructed his followers at a public meeting that if they were to spot a Brahmin and a snake together, the Brahmin was to be dealt with first. The dream of the Brahmins who got left behind in Tamil Nadu was to somehow reach the shores of America. Thus, Brahmins began disowning Tamil and English assumed primacy in their lives. A community which was at the very apex of the social strata severed itself from Tamil society. Fifty years ago, except for a few, all Tamil writers were Brahmins!

Now, we come to the role of Tamil films and its extension, television. Dravidian leaders like Annadurai and Karunanidhi entered politics through films, and Karunanidhi still remains reasonably active in Tamil filmdom. During his stint as Chief Minister between 2006 and 2011 he continued to essay dialogues and scripts for films. Not a day ended without him attending a film-based event. Nowhere would you probably see a society so obsessed with films. A friend who is a professor of French in Chennai was teaching her students the intricacies of the usage of prepositions in the language. When she asked a student to use the appropriate preposition for China, the student was unsure whether China was a town or a country. My friend observed that the same student possessed a staggering level of knowledge about film stars and their personal lives.

Another friend who edits a Tamil magazine, once received a parcel containing a severed human finger floating in a jar of formaldehyde. An accompanying letter from its sender said that he was hoping to be written about in the magazine which could be a ticket to meet a certain film star he worshipped. Then, there was a moron who cut off his tongue and offered it to Lord Venkateshwara of Tirupati so that his leader would win the election.

Camp and uncouthness now define Tamil popular culture. Here is a sampler. In a movie from a couple of years ago, where one of Karunanidhi's grandsons plays the lead, a scene goes like this: The hero riding a two-wheeler stops at a traffic signal and looks at a girl whose face is covered with a dupatta. The hero tries to make a move on her. When the girl removes her veil to reveal her "unattractive" face (made worse by buck teeth), the hero spits on the ground in a display of revulsion and contempt for her. I cannot imagine a film elsewhere in the world containing such a sickening scene. Probably a Kim Ki Duk film might have such a sequence, but surely the man indulging in the act would perhaps be portrayed as a psycho or a sadist. In our case here, he is the adorable hero; even a prospective Chief Minister.

The propensity of Tamils to offer ritual libations of milk and honey (now beer, in keeping with postmodern times) to the plywood cutouts of stars and politicians is deserving of a serious sociological study. This culture of cutout *abhishekam* is yet another gift of the Dravidian parties to the Tamil society. Every actor has a fan club and the members of these fan clubs find themselves as vice-chancellors of universities and college deans, when their hero becomes a power player. In any country, the state of universities and media are the barometers of cultural and societal maturity. But in Tamil Nadu, these two institutions serve as an everyday reminder of our cultural philistinism.

In magazines, a majority of the pages are crammed with cinema news; essays and columns are written by film lyricists; questions pour in for reader Q&A sections anchored by directors; and pictures of half-naked female actors can be found in every alternate page. The pages that are left are filled with pictures of woe-stricken Sri Lankan Tamils. Since most of the university vice-chancellors were errand boys of the film-star-turned-CMs, they indulge actors, directors and sundry celebrities by decorating them with honorary doctorates. Writers and intellectuals are damned. This class has to face disrespect and derision on a daily basis.

A few years ago, a well-known French writer and I were invited to deliver a speech at a leading university in Tamil Nadu. We were ushered in to the VC's office for a courtesy visit. The VC said he knew of me through my television appearances. During our 30 minute interaction, he showed no inclination to know about our works. He was keen on doing all the talking. What is more, he would often pat the Frenchman on his thigh as though they were bosom buddies. My flustered friend felt that this kind of behavior would be frowned upon even at a bar table among friends, let alone strangers. For half an hour, it felt like I was in a conversation with an unlettered auto rickshaw driver, not a VC of a university.

Robert Bresson made a movie based on Dostoevsky's

Gentle Creature in 1969. The hero, a middle aged money lender marries a poor girl. The girl is portrayed as being interested in Shakespeare and ornithology. The same novel was adapted for a recent film called With You, Without You by a Sri Lankan director called Prasanna Vithanage. Here, the heroine is a poor Tamil girl who is married to a Sri Lankan money lender. In a telling comment on contemporary Tamil society, the perceptive director shows the girl's sole ambition in life as travelling to Tamil Nadu and meeting her matinee idol Vijay. Tamils living in any part of the world are the same. Only, for some, Vijay can be replaced by an Ajith, Kamal Haasan or Rajnikanth.

The precise cultural difference between the Tamils and rest of the world is this; how can I as a creator of literary fiction, given this state of affairs and social milieu, reach a wider audience? Only translation could help; but we have a dearth of readers, forget competent translators. A friend of mine from north India publishes an English literary magazine where writers from everywhere write. Except for a few original pieces in English, the rest are translations from Indian and foreign languages. I eagerly scanned the magazine for translations from Tamil. I was amazed to find a translation of Andal, the ninth century *bhakti* poet, by a Tamil who works at a Japanese University as an English professor. If a contemporary literary magazine is only just publishing the translation of a ninth century poet, how many centuries will I have to wait to get my works translated?

September 16, 2014

THE ANGEL OF JUSTICE IN JAIL

The completely unchecked and loathsome hooliganism of ADMK supporters, post Jayalalitha's conviction, makes us wonder if we really live in a republic. The AIADMK cadres and functionaries are conveniently forgetting the fact that their supremom has been convicted for the inordinate assets she unlawfully owned between 1991 and 1996. It has been proved in court that Jayalalitha's assets were worth Rs.2 crore in 1991, which surged up to Rs.60 crore in a span of few years, while her fellow convicts were drawing an annual income less than Rs.1 lakh during the same year. When a charge was filed against this, Jayalalitha and her confidante, Sasikala, resorted to dilatory tactics, forcing a delay of 18 years for the verdict to be pronounced.

Since the day of the verdict, citizens are witnessing strange, uncivil and shameful events in Tamil Nadu. The state of affairs that prevailed on the day of the verdict reminded me of 2 February, 2000, when Jayalalitha was sentenced to a year's imprisonment in another case. Consequently, her party men set fire to a college bus in Dharmapuri with students inside and burnt three girls alive to ashes.

Of course, no one can forget the atrocious governance the state witnessed during the previous DMK regime.

The people loathed the DMK to the core and thus, gave Jayalalitha a sweeping victory in the 2011 polls. Anyone contemplating the political scenario of Tamil Nadu since 1967, can easily discern that the Tamils have an attitude of voting in favour of opposition parties. And thus, Karunanidhi and Jayalalitha alternately kept making it to Fort St. George, uncompeted.

But people detested the Karunanidhi government in 2011 like never before. Massive corruption and unforeseen power shortages were the order of the day. Rowdyism was taken to extremes, where DMK bullies dared to slap policemen inside their stations. Since those troublemakers were big shots in the party, the khaki-clads had to endure all this with folded hands. In the meantime, Tamil Nadu had to relive the Middle Ages, when electricity had not yet been discovered. While other districts saw unannounced and erratic power failures, the capital city went electrically sterile for at least three hours every day. Before the 2011 polls, I predicted that the DMK would barely win 30 constituencies, while most of the opinion polls were in favour of the party. (Cho Ramasway's *Thuglak* was, of course, an exception.)

Predictably, Jayalalitha came to power and her government initially lived up to the taxpayers' expectations. For instance, they gradually resolved the power crisis. But sadly, she started on her road to perdition when she chose her rival, Karunanidhi, as her role model. Had she been following the proven model of Narendra Modi in Gujarat instead, the stars would have continued to favour her. Her government continued endorsing alcoholism by increasing the number of TASMAC liquor shops in every nook and cranny of the state. She granted freebies to people, double of what the DMK government had done. My personal opinion is that Jayalalitha's government managed to encourage—even delight—drunkards and lazy good-for-nothings allergic to labour and addicted to freebies in these three years, though the trend was started by the earlier regime.

At this juncture, I am deeply worried about the plight of Tamil Nadu. The activities of ADMK supporters, post the conviction of their chief, are loathsome and highly condemnable. To watch the governments at the Centre and the State do nothing to restore law and order in the State, is to wonder if I really live in a republic. On 27 September, offices were shut down at noon and I saw women literally running back to their homes. Shops pulled their shutters down and the State only had the ADMK men with their flagpoles in the streets. I call this an undeclared curfew. Once the court declared Jayalalitha guilty, transportation services were disrupted and buses were burnt. The only consolation was that this time, the buses were empty.

Since the day she was taken to task, the assembly members of ADMK and their ministers keep protesting in various ways to get their party chief released. They call for hunger strikes and also pressure corporates to join their protests. It is bewildering to hear education personnel announce arbitrarily that the schools in the State will not function for a day. Roadways are disconnected despite the

Dussehra festivities and people were scared to even step out of their homes. Adding fuel to the fire, emotionally distraught ADMK representatives are abusing the Kannadigas in Tamil Nadu thereby, inviting danger to the thousands of Tamils living in Bengaluru.

To object to a court's verdict is a punishable offense under 'contempt of court'. So I am surprised to see that the Indian Penal Code is keeping mum when contempt of court is done in groups and masses. This strange state of affairs in Tamil Nadu raises a question about whether there is a license to do anything unlawful provided it is in groups.

And Jayalalitha has not been convicted for being a social activist, unlike Irom Sharmila and Aung San Suu Kyi. It was the talk of the town during the 1990s that Jayalalitha volunteered to receive a salary of just one rupee during her first tenure. And it was during the same period she was found possessing assets worth ₹60 crore. Strange, illogical, ironical, or whatever, it is insulting and humiliating to the old man who lived like a mendicant fakir in the same nation, wearing barely a loincloth.

But I find a lot of people, including my friends, sympathizing for Jayalalitha. They tend to defend her, comparing her case with Karunanidhi's 2G scandal. This attitude of the masses proves that the Tamils have lost all their virtues. Kamaraj, Kakkan and Rajaji ruled the same State; their hands were unstained. Kamaraj's bank balance was some hundred rupees when he passed away. But today, corruption has become the lifestyle—these waves of sympathy are proof of this.

At the same time, I find this verdict a positive sign in Indian politics. I appreciate Justice Michael D'Cunha for his uncompromising gesture. While dirty politicians find this alarming, the country's youth find this verdict promising and encouraging. The youngsters are allergic to corruption, which the recent Parliament polls proved magnificently. Now they have something to pin their hopes on, after all.

This scenario is very new to Tamil Nadu politics. While people have never forgotten the 2G scandal, the BJP garnered no advantage from this. The party lacks eminent leaders to win the lower class votes. Its state leader apparently visited Rajinikanth's residence this Dussehra.

"Injustice to the angel of justice?", "Could earthly bodies punish heavenly bodies?" I have roughly translated to English, the ridiculous Tamil slogans painted on the walls of Chennai with huge pictures of Jayalalitha.

And I am scared to have my wife read this space. "Are you inviting ADMK enmity too?," she would yell at me for sure. I had to confront threats to my life during the DMK regime, for my political columns. I am unsure of the toll that I will have to pay this time.

October 9, 2014

NOT MUCH TO CHOOSE FROM
FOR VOTERS IN TN POLLS

Tamil Nadu's current socio-political and cultural status is ripe madness. For the next 10 years, the people of Tamil Nadu cannot forget the era of darkness they witnessed between 2006 and 2011. That is because for five years, they experienced 18 to 20 hour power blackouts every single day. No one, not even the media, really cared about this parlous state of affairs. Newspaper presses, television studios and software parks ran on diesel gensets. No one cared.

The then chief minister M. Karunanidhi believed he was destined by divine fate to occupy that chair for ever. Such hubris made him shun matters of governance, and focus completely on things like writing scripts for films, coming up with cheap puns in the Tamil language, and leading a fun life in general. When the war in Sri Lanka against the Tamil rebels was reaching its climax, Karunanidhi embarked on a world famous two hour fast 'unto death' at the Marina Beach. Not surprisingly, the voters rejected the DMK, pushing the party to the third place in the state.

Except M.G. Ramachandran, no chief minister could tide over anti-incumbency. People have overwhelmingly rejected the ruling party during elections. They do not vote for the opposition because of the trust or faith they have in them to be a good governance alternative. For instance, in 2011, it was a vote against the 18-20 hour power cuts that DMK forced on people, rather than a positive mandate for AIADMK. This is how the AIADMK and DMK have been sharing power in Tamil Nadu.

Campaigning for elections has ended. The state-owned TASMAC liquor shops will not open for the next three days. You simply cannot discuss Tamil Nadu politics without talking about TASMAC. In developed countries, the State provides quality education and healthcare. In Tamil Nadu however, the media and politicians have successfully sold the myth that enforcing prohibition would transform people's lives rather than the delivery of quality education or healthcare.

If you are a regular drinker in Tamil Nadu, death on account of liver failure is almost certain. That is because of the adulterated alcohol that TASMAC sells, distilled and brewed in the factories owned by DMK and AIADMK stalwarts. The liquor barons do not need to worry about which party comes to power. No other state buys the adulterated hooch made in Tamil Nadu. With the State running the alcohol procurement and retail business without any room for private participation, there is no concept or need of quality control. Except AIADMK, all parties have promised that prohibition is the first policy they would implement if voted to power. Here, all laws are visible only on paper. Good luck to those who believe that these politicians would truly enforce such a law.

Chief minister Jayalalitha resembles the unbelievable

characters of Roald Dahl's novels. She flew from venue to venue in a helicopter. To avoid using the chopper at night, she usually addressed rallies at three in the afternoon. For that, the hired crowd would be shepherded in at nine am. Local party functionaries were given numerical targets of the number of people each had to bring in. For standing in the 40-degree heat from nine in the morning to six in the evening, these poor people were paid Rs.300. They had no access to drinking water or bathroom facilities. They stood barefoot at these rallies. Scores of people collapsed, unable to cope with the oppressive conditions. Six people died from the heat at her meetings. On the other hand, the CM's stage always had eight air conditioners and six air coolers.

There is not much to say about the DMK. A longtime party sympathizer told me recently, that the Karunanidhi family will not be satisfied even if you gifted them the entire state.

However, the biggest tragedy of this election is what passes for the 'third front'. It is actually a tragicomedy. The Pattali Makkal Katchi (PMK) has often opportunistically piggybacked on DMK and AIADMK. That is the reason why voters refuse to trust the party when it is contesting on its own, without aligning with any of the two big parties. Also, the PMK is finding it hard to shed the image of being a Vanniyar caste group party. Like most other political parties in India, the PMK is accursed by dynastic politics. PMK founder Ramadoss had once said that if he or the members of his family ever occupied public office, the citizens could flog him in a public square. Now, Ramadoss wants his son Anbumani to become the CM.

In the last elections, people bestowed upon Vijayakanth, the honour of being the principal leader of opposition. But he did not even go to the legislative assembly often enough to speak about people's issues. Vijayakanth's histrionics have been truly bizarre. From sticking his tongue out at a public meeting as a gesture of threat, to thrashing his own candidates, to spitting on journalists, the actor-turned-politician has broken every convention of public decency.

Vijayakanth became a celluloid hero on the back of dialogues written by scriptwriters. In political life however, when he has to write his own lines, he has turned into a comedian. A case in point is the interview he gave NDTV's Prannoy Roy. Not being fluent in English is not a crime. But why not have the common sense to engage an interpreter when appearing on national television? 'I am hero, Karunanidhi is a villain, Jayalalitha villi.' is the kind of incoherent nonsense which he has made his signature.

Then we have minor sideshows and newcomers such as Seeman, a cine-director-turned-politician and founder of the Naam Thamizhar Party. In the next 10 years, he is going to become a social menace. His public speaking style seems heavily influenced by Hitler. Like Hitler, he is spreading dubious racist theories among the youth. His brand of Tamil chauvinist politics is extremely dangerous. When I listen to Seeman's speeches, I feel like slashing my wrist. He recently declared that it was not the Sinhalese who carried out the genocide of Tamil in Sri Lanka, but the Telugu speaking Nayakars. If you are wondering how, think Sinhala names such as Bandaranayake, Senanayake etc. According to Seeman's worldview, they were all Telugu Nayakars.

This is the choice that the people of Tamil Nadu have before them today. But then, people deserve the politicians they get.

May 14, 2016

IF MY SUPERSTAR'S FILM FLOPS, I'LL JUMP INTO
FIRE

In the recently concluded assembly elections in Tamil Nadu, the one loud call we heard from multiple quarters was: 'O people, don't take money from politicians to sell your vote.' Let us look at those who issued this clarion call. First, there was the Election Commission, then, film actors, public intellectuals and media organizations. The Election Commission had lost all moral authority to say this. In these elections, the EC was not a watchdog. It performed the role of a passive observer. One wonders if this was indeed the institution that somebody like T.N. 'Alsatian' Seshan once helmed. Film stars who command nothing less than Rs.10-20 crore for a movie have an even lesser moral case to make against citizens taking a vote-bribe. This is not a diatribe against my 'Superstar'. Who, you ask. For me, there is only one 'Superstar' in the world!

If you look at the people employed in the marginal sectors - the municipal workers, fuel station attendants, or gas cylinder delivery men, or even the daily wage, temporary staffers employed by the state government - they subsist on an average monthly wage of Rs.4,000 or thereabouts. In the postal department where I worked for several years, there were thousands of temps earning Rs.200 a day. Slightly higher on the pyramid are school teachers whose monthly income ranges from Rs.5,000 to Rs.15,000.

The primary objective of the urban poor is somehow turning their progeny into trees that yield money. Even before the child comes out of the mother's womb, they start planning for the upkeep of this 'cash crop'. That is because you need to cough up Rs.5 lakh (in cash, without receipt) just for an admission to play schools these days. With expensive private education being a distant dream, this is how a typical low income group parent thinks: 'Because I don't have the money, I've put my child in a corporation school. My son is pure as a bar of gold. He was once suspended for beating up his teacher, but otherwise he has managed to keep away from any hanky-panky, unlike my friends' kids. Some of them, even at this young age go to the extent of molesting their teachers under the influence of alcohol and land themselves in juvenile homes. When he finishes school, I somehow need to rustle up the Rs.5 lakh to send him to Dubai. Once that happens, I can buy two houses here. Then life would be a breeze. I hear there are lots of Malayalees in Dubai. That shouldn't be a problem. He can pick up the language doubly quick at the neighbourhood Nair's tea shop.'

The middle class holds a slightly different view on the matter. The money spent on children is an investment. Poor return on investment (RoI) is intolerable. 'How can you not study hard when I'm spending so much,' goes the usual refrain. Money is the basis of life. Everything can be bought. Money can open the doors of heaven. School is merely a place that trains you to make money. The lot of girl children in middle class homes is even worse.

June after June, the front pages of Tamil newspapers are filled with mug shots of district, zone, state topping girls. Whatever happens to them after a few years? Inevitably, they turn into idli-dosa makers and child bearers for the male, money minting machines. If you ask me, I would say educating girls is a useless exercise.

In short, in the modern Tamil life, money not only lends meaning, but also determines the worth of all human activity. That being the case, is it not absurd to tell us not to take money?

You may have heard of Tiruvalluvar. He divided life into *aram* (wisdom), *porul* (the material) and *inbam* (love). We Tamils continue to follow Tiruvalluvar, but have tweaked his teachings to suit our times and mores. We have fused wisdom and the material. We pray to God for the material, and hope that He retains the wisdom bit. That is why temples these days, especially those renowned for wish-granting powers, are chock-a-block. What about love? I feel queasy saying this, but let me say it anyway. That is available on a 70mm screen in a dark cinema hall where the 60-year-old hero cavorts with a 16-year-old girl in snowy Switzerland (so what if he's 60? The artiste never ages!).

Very soon, on 1 July, if all goes well, our Superstar's next film releases. Just thinking about it gives me gooseflesh. There is work to be done in readiness for D-Day. Giant 60-feet cutouts of the 'Leader' have to be erected. Earlier, we would bathe the giant plywood likenesses of our God in milk. The times, they are a-changin. Now, amber beer is the preferred beverage for *abhishekam*. The film will be a guaranteed hit, unlike the last two guaranteed hits that flopped. In the unlikely event of it bombing at the box office, I shall immolate myself.

The act of self-immolation is the proud heritage of the Tamil race. In days past, we set ourselves on fire to fight the imposition of Hindi. Now we do it when our Dear Leaders are inconvenienced - sent to jail for corruption. When Jayalalitha was sent to jail once, a bus was torched and three college girls were charred to death. Then there was this guy who chopped off his tongue and dropped it off in the Tirupati *hundi* when Amma once lost an election. I know you readers in other states must be wrinkling your noses. Listen, we are a passionate people. Stuff happens in moments of frenzy.

But then, did Amma not reward him suitably with cash for his great penance?

I merely follow in the footsteps of my illustrious fellow Tamils. Ergo, if my Superstar's film flops, I shall lunge into the inferno.

Postscript: Do not think this the rant of an illiterate. I have a PhD on the films of 'Superstar'. When he does indeed enter politics, I shall be made the vice-chancellor of a university in Tamil Nadu. Beware!

May 17, 2016

JAYALALITHA SHOULD UNDERSTAND THE DISSENT OF THE COMMON MAN

Tamil Nadu witnessed a strange election this year. After 1984, the mandate was always against the incumbent government. But this year, the anti-incumbency wave was on par with the people's hatred towards the DMK. With the exception to the Amma Mess - an *Idli* for a rupee and tomato rice for five rupees - the State machinery was inactive for the most part of the past five years. The December, 2015 Chennai deluge was the highest point of inaction of the AIADMK administration. The bureaucracy could not contact Jayalalitha during the Chennai deluge. Had an IAS acted on his own to contain the floods from Chembarambakkam without a yes from Jayalalitha, he would have earned Jayalalitha's wrath. Even a central minister said he could not get Jayalalitha's appointment. She remained inaccessible to the common man, the press, the Central Minister and the state bureaucracy.

The AIADMK ministers on the other hand, were busy on a pilgrimage hopping from one temple to another, tonsuring their heads, thus, having no time to hear people's concerns. The mandate would certainly be against the incumbent government in such a political scenario.

But, the citizenry was disillusioned against both the AIADMK and the DMK, and was willing to give the third front, a chance. To their dismay, they could not discover a viable third front. Unfortunately, it was Mr Vijayakanth, a buffoon in disguise, who was the CM candidate of the third front. He pushed the DMK to the third place in the 2011 elections and was the Opposition leader. He wasted a golden opportunity; his attendance was poor in the Assembly. His public acts were unbecoming of a leader; his histrionics have been truly bizarre. From sticking his tongue out at public meeting as a gesture of threat, to thrashing his own candidates, to spitting on journalists, the actor-turned-politician has broken every convention of public decency. He never seemed to understand the difference between reel and real life.

The citizenry could not accept the leadership of Mr Thirumavalavan either, because caste hierarchy and untouchability is still rooted in their minds. The Dalits invariably remain pawns in both the DMK and the AIADMK. The Pattali Makkal Katchi has a long way ahead to shed its image of being a caste outfit. PMK's chief ministerial candidate, Dr Anbumani, did not realize that Kaduvetti Guru's hate speech towards the Dalits brought a bad repute to the PMK. He should also understand that prohibition and development are two different wor(l)ds.

Unlike other leaders, Dr Anbumani had toured many foreign nations. There is no proof in history that prohibition leads to development. The deaths caused by the TASMAC liquor are because of the poor quality of liquor brewed in the distilleries owned by the heavyweights of the AIADMK and the DMK. How can you explain the lesser number of liquor related deaths in Karnataka? Quality education, quality health care, better roads - these should be the priority of a welfare State. The roads of Tamil Nadu are in a bad shape, reminding us of the Middle Ages. Both education and health care vary in quality to the poor and the elite. With the kind of education that a poor person gets in Tamil Nadu, he can only become an auto driver.

Both the DMK and the AIADMK have a strong vote bank in Tamil Nadu. Their loyalists will always vote for their respective parties, no matter how poor their rule. Barring these sympathizers, everyone - from an auto driver to an IT employee - longed for a Kejriwal. Tamil Nadu needs an incorruptible leader, they said. You can speak of Mr Nallakannu of the CPI. But the fact that the Communists allied either with the DMK or the AIADMK in the previous elections, deterred the people away from them. One should not forget that Mr Nallakannu is also a marginalised person, who needs a leader. Gandhian austerity and a simple dhoti alone do not make one a leader. One should fight for the cause of the common man. Sadly, the Communists have a long road ahead before they even think of it.

The results were nail-biting, resembling a T20 match, switching the wind in favour of the DMK and the AIADMK until the last ball. After the 1984 elections, no ruling party regained power successively. This time, the AIADMK belied all the pre-polls and exit polls. But in reality, the majority of the votes got by the AIADMK were not positive votes. The common man could not find an alternative to the AIADMK. He did not forget the grotesque 2006-2011 DMK reign. Had he forgotten or forgiven, the common man would have voted the DMK to power. A positive note for the DMK bastion is that they have grown into a strong Opposition now.

The greatest loser this time is the third front, headed by Mr Vijayakanth. He lost his status as the Opposition leader now, because he lacked leadership qualities. He learnt the hard way that he cannot become a Karunanidhi. His DMDK MLAs were given a run for their money by Jayalalitha. They could not answer her questions during the debates in the Assembly. Both the DMDK and AIADMK MLAs were similar when it comes to expertise in public matters. At the least, Jayalalitha wields control over her party MPs in Delhi. She has taught the 37 MPs when to speak and when to remain silent in the Parliament. Vijayakanth, on the other hand, lacks this art of handling a remote control.

The prohibition promise made by the DMK, the PMK and the third front proved to be a laughable farce. That the prohibition is the biggest issue in the State, was a myth created by a section of the media. One has to remember that Jayalalitha never promised a total prohibition.

And now that the results have come, with the DMK going to be a powerful Opposition, Jayalalitha should understand the dissent of the common man. The take-home point for Jayalalitha should be this: Stop the freebies and thrive hard to improve the standard of living of the common man.

May 19, 2016

JAYALALITHA SHOULD THANK STALIN MORE THAN VOTERS

Jayalalitha thanked the people of Tamil Nadu for keeping her in office. She actually should have thanked arch rival DMK's treasurer MK Stalin. It was Stalin who nixed all chances of Vijayakanth allying with the DMK. Stalin literally drove him away. Vijayakanth had demanded some 70 seats, which DMK chief Karunanidhi was more than willing to accommodate. For the sake of the alliance Karunanidhi, the senior most active politician in the land, had set aside his ego. This shows Stalin does not even possess a fraction of his father's political acumen.

However, there's another way of looking at the Tamil Nadu election results - from Stalin's own point of view - that would make him look like a Machiavellian genius. Put yourselves in Stalin shoes for a minute, and this is how it would play out: "If I hadn't shut the door on Vijayakanth, DMK would have returned to power and daddy would have had the distinction of being the oldest CM at the age of 93. I am 63 already. If daddy ruled for five years, I'd be 68 by the time next elections happen. Given Tamil Nadu's tradition of booting out the incumbent government, the soonest DMK could hope to win an election would be 2026. How old would I be then? I'm weak in math. I should ask daddy. Despite doing yoga and walking in the mornings, such complex calculations make me huff and puff. But today, I've accomplished what I wanted. So what if I can't become the CM, at least the party would be under my complete control."

It is not hard to imagine Karunanidhi being livid at Stalin for denying him the epochal opportunity to become CM at 93.

If you look at the AIADMK, the party men are celebrating the victory in utter disbelief.

Jayalalitha's statement post the win is a bit worrying. She has promised to fulfil each one of her election promises. These promises are nothing but freebies that would encourage the poor to remain happy with economic status quo in their lives. What are these freebies? Mixer-grinder, sewing machine, laptop, 8 grams of gold for mangalsutra, 50% cheaper two wheelers and so on. The list is endless. The freebies are not going to change the quality of life. People in the state still run from pillar to post carrying plastic pots looking for drinking water. The quality of education is pathetic. Public healthcare remains weak. Instead of lavishing more freebies, Jayalalitha would do well to implement some good ideas from the PMK manifesto about high-quality universal education and healthcare.

There are two other very important things Jayalalitha must do at once. She needs to do away with her circle of slaves who perpetually prostrate before her and induct responsible and competent individuals in key positions. She needs to understand that those constantly venerating are neck deep in corruption. For example, her MLAs bang the benches cheering every single word she utters inside the assembly. Jaya TV then dutifully makes a newsreel out of it. It is one of the most vulgar sights you can encounter.

I see both AIADMK and DMK, culturally as one. There is hardly anything to differentiate their delusions of grandeur when in power. During DMK's rule, when one of Karunanidhi's grandchildren got married, there were giant cut-outs all over the city and some 5000 flex advertising boards installed. With the AIADMK in power for five more years, expect to see more images of Jayalalitha as Virgin Mary, Durga, and many other divine avatars.

There's a small bit of personal satisfaction, however, with the AIADMK's victory. My physical safety is guaranteed because no one in the party reads literature. Since Karunanidhi himself is a writer, the party remains in touch with writers and intellectuals. Anticipating a DMK win, I had started practising using the Indian style toilets. You need some practice in case you had to spend some time in the jail. Now for the next five years, I needn't fear that eventuality. I've happily switched back to the WC.

May 20, 2016

WHEN THE REEL HERO CAN'T
KEEP IT REAL

———

I did not want to write on l'affaire actor Suriya and his roadside 'heroics' especially when the matter is under police investigation. However, I do wish to talk about our collective attitudes towards people who happen to look dark, and apparently poor.

A luxury car crosses the Adyar Bridge in Chennai. There's a 21-year-old boy on a motorbike just behind the car. The car brakes suddenly. The bike crashes into the car. The woman driving the car gets into a heated argument with the biker. Traffic gets stalled. There are plenty of fruit and flower shops by the roadside there. A few women selling flowers step in to diffuse the tension. Just then, Kollywood star Suriya, passing by, stops his car, gets down and thrashes the young man. The biker asks Suriya why he was raining blows on him when it was the woman driving the car who was at fault. Without any explanation, Suriya reportedly sped away. Suriya may have thought that the young man was harassing a woman. Or, as Suriya claims, he may just have tried to mediate between the two jousting parties. But that is the job of the police. Let's look at how social and police psychology works in such cases.

The young man in question is dark complexioned; he looks poor. Our social reflex is to turn violent when we encounter such people who we believe are in the wrong. The young man bravely approaches the police. Even after waiting for a couple of hours, his complaint against Suriya is not accepted. It finally is, when lawyers associated with human rights groups turn up. Even after that, it is only the boy and not Suriya who is repeatedly questioned by the police.

Intimidated, the boy says he fears the police would beat him death, or in the face of such humiliation, he'd commit suicide.

My question is simply this: If there is a traffic-related fracas (and it's all too common in our cities), is it more appropriate to try and calm down the warring parties and resolve the matter amicably rather than mix the reel and real and get into roadside fisticuffs to save a 'damsel in distress'? That the dark man ought to be the villain is Kollywood logic. Going by that logic, the majority of people in India are worthy of a good pummelling.

If it's indeed true that actor Suriya had hit the young man, he must apologise and recompense him for the physical and mental inconvenience he has suffered. It needn't prick his ego, especially because he also tries hard to wear the hat of a philanthropist.

Some months ago, when the Chennai Metro was being inaugurated, DMK bigwig Stalin decided to take a train ride and mingle with the masses. He allegedly slapped a young man who tried to touch him. A video capturing the incident surfaced on social media platforms. However, the youngster at the receiving end claimed that 'thalapathi' Stalin hadn't slapped him but merely patted him asking him to give way. The list of people Vijayakanth has manhandled is too long to be enumerated in this column. Our celebrities and high-profile politicians are distinctly uncomfortable in the midst of hoi polloi. They prefer keeping a distance of a few feet from the common folk in public appearances. When they do choose to mix with us, violence often ensues. This is the kind of society we live in.

June 1, 2016

JAYALALITHA

When thinking of J Jayalalitha's life, the image that flashes first is from a Tamil Nadu Assembly session on March 25, 1989. The Opposition leader then, she was physically attacked by members of the ruling Dravida Munnetra Kazhagam, right before the speaker's eyes and at the provocation of M Karunanidhi, who was chief minister at the time. She came out of the Assembly with her sari torn. That incident generated a massive sympathy wave for Jayalalitha.

In Tamil Nadu, the creation of a leader and the amount of trust the voters place on them is purely a function of the grudge they bear against the ruling party. The only two exceptions to this rule were K Kamaraj of the Congress and MG Ramachandran.

In that way, Jayalalitha owes a lot of her initial popularity to Karunanidhi. The other reason why she captured a firm place in the minds of people were the events in the immediate aftermath of MGR's death in December 1987. For several hours after her mentor's death, she was the only person to be seen standing beside MGR's body. Millions of people watched those images on television. However, she was later literally kicked out of the open-top hearse.

For someone who came into public life riding on

a political wave of epic proportions, the first signs of disenchantment appeared in 1992 when the Kumbakonam temple stampede occurred during the Mahamakam festival. It was an avoidable tragedy. Chief Minister Jayalalitha and her friend Sasikala went to the temple tank for a holy dip when there were thousands of other pilgrims. For her security, the authorities sealed off the northern and southern approaches and exits from the tank. This led to the death of 50 people, while many others were injured.

Close on the heels of the Mahamakam tragedy came the disastrous wedding of Jayalalitha's foster son VN Sudhakaran – a relative of Sasikala – in 1995. Its brazen opulence and scale would have put any medieval sultan to shame. The wedding made it to the Guinness Book of World Records on two counts: for being the wedding with the biggest guest list and for feeding an unprecedented number of people.

Several photographs from the wedding contributed to public opinion on Jayalalitha turning viciously hostile. The most egregious was one of Jayalalitha and Sasikala bedecked in more gold than you would find in an entire jewellery megastore.

Adopted by Jayalalitha in 1995, Sudhakaran was disowned by her a year later. Those events contributed immensely to her crushing electoral defeat in 1996. Subsequently, a case of heroin possession was slapped against the foster son, and he even had to go to jail.

In 2000, when Jayalalitha was sentenced to jail for

owning assets disproportionate to her income, workers of her party, the All India Anna Dravida Munnetra Kazhagam, set fire to a bus in Dharmapuri, killing three college girls. That is yet another incident from the leader's long political life that people are unlikely to forget easily.

Since Jayalalitha was admitted to the Apollo Hospital on September 22 this year, there has been an element of fear among the public. In 2014, during her incarceration at a Bengaluru prison after her conviction in the wealth amassment case, it felt like the lumpen were running affairs in Tamil Nadu. Nobody could control anybody. Even before the ink on her conviction had dried, shops had downed shutters. Those that didn't were ransacked by her supporters.

Karunanidhi is the pioneer of such use of muscle power. In July 1971, Karunanidhi, who was then the chief minister, was conferred an honorary doctorate by Annamalai University in Chidambaram. Protesting the decision, a section of students paraded a donkey around campus with a board around its neck that read "doctor". The police stormed the hostel and brutally thrashed the students. The next day, the body of one student, Udayakumar, was found floating in a pond on campus. The police denied his identity. Intimidated by the police, even Udayakumar's parents denied his death.

In the last 45 years, three politicians – MGR, Karunanidhi and Jayalalitha – have had the biggest influence on the history and lives of the Tamil people. Jayalalitha's maiden speech as a Rajya Sabha member in the 1980s marked her out as remarkably intelligent and unusually well-read among contemporary Tamil politicians.

There was mild consternation about the prospect of a Brahmin Jayalalitha infusing a flavour of English education into the culture of Dravidian politics. All such fears were misplaced. The same Jayalalitha ushered in the by now commonplace but cringe-inducing practice of ministers and apparatchiks falling at her feet.

Jayalalitha had led a lonely life for a very long time. She lost her father at the age of two. She grew up in Bengaluru, living with her aunt till she was 10. That was when her mother, Vedavalli, was working in the Chennai film industry under the screen name Sandhya. It was only after she reached the age of 10 that Jayalalitha started living with her mother. She has spoken about this in the television show Rendezvous with Simi Garewal. During her childhood, it was her mother who controlled Jayalalitha's life. Later, it was MGR, and finally the Mannargudi group or the Sasikala family.

Jayalalitha has followed in the footsteps of Karunanidhi when it comes to politics. She should have learnt some lessons on living a long life as well from her bête noire. After turning 60, Karunanidhi started learning yoga under TKV Desikachar. But Jayalalitha's doctors had to be those related to Sasikala.

In the last 45 years, the standards of education or healthcare among the poor of Tamil Nadu have remained pretty much the same. Jayalalitha ensured that the poor did not, at least, die of hunger. Her much vaunted Amma Canteens serve food for as little as Rs 5. The state's people settled for cheap food and assorted freebies over meaningful development.

I recently watched the TV series Narcos on the life of Colombian drug lord Pablo Escobar. If you take out the killings, Narcos is pretty much the story of Tamil Nadu politics. Every councillor or local body leader in the state is a mini Escobar. The rule of law is subservient to their whims and ambitions. It is a myth that the police are more empowered during Jayalalitha's rule. The spate of murders in all the state's major cities proves that. You can trace almost every murder to a councillor or the land mafia – and in most cases, the two are the same.

How was the life of the average Tamil in the last 10 years, six of those under Jayalalitha's rule?

The loneliness that accompanied her childhood was once again a constant feature of her life in her final 10 years. It is inconceivable that the Mannargudi gang could have helped her overcome this loneliness.

Tamil Nadu, too, suffered the effects of Jayalalitha's loneliness. How else do we even try to make sense of O Panneerselvam's interim chief ministership? Is it possible that one woman's angst and angularities shape the course of a democratic society in this fashion in the 21st century?

We, the people, are mere props in this fairytale of epic proportions.

December 6, 2016

A DANGEROUS BRAND OF
FASCISM

There are two extreme and opposing positions when it comes to national symbols. Some make a case for a European approach where flag-waving nationalism is frowned upon (with exceptions made for football matches) while others link extreme piety for every national symbol to patriotism.

In the West, it's common for celebrities and sportstars to pose for photographs wearing undergarments in the colours of the national flag. Religious icons figure in popular songs laden with sexual innuendo. For a long time, it has been fashionable to ape the West. Could we copy them in this regard as well? I feel it is quite impossible. India has worshipped trees, rivers, the sun, and the earth we live on since the ancient times. The elders in my village would admonish children for urinating on tree trunks. Trees are deemed divine. The Indian tradition treats the earth as mother. To try and use Western frameworks to understand Indian life would be futile.

There is bound to be a difference in how the West influences our minds and Indian minds' attitude towards national symbols. Can Indians think of wearing flip-flops with the Indian flag printed on it?

In the Mahabharata, Hanuman graced Arjuna's chariot

flag. It was Hanuman's promise to the Pandavas that he'd be with them throughout war and help them.

For a people whose tradition teaches them the value of symbols such as flags, it would be inconceivable to denigrate them by sporting them on shoes or undergarments.

But in the name of guarding our traditions, the thought process of Indians is slowly but surely being directed towards fascism.

At the recent Chennai Film Festival, I happened to watch five films in a day and had to stand up for the national anthem each time a film began. The screening at one of the theatres had to be stopped because some tried to rough up a group of women who hadn't bothered to stand up for the anthem.

This heady cocktail of Hindutva and ultra-nationalism seeks to chip away at our great diversity. Unlike China, and other modern Western nation states, there is no cultural, racial, or linguistic homogeneity in India. India has countless languages, dialects, ethnicities and cultural traditions. In our diversity lies our greatness. The forces of Hindutva-hypernationalism seek to flatten out this diverse landscape. They realize that mere slogans won't help them achieve their objective. They need everyday rituals to constantly reinforce their message. The forcible worship of national symbols are those rituals.

Incidents such as the molestation of a Bengaluru woman on New Year's Eve, and the attack on women in theatres for not standing up for the national anthem are closely connected. In the worldview of those who unleash such violence, the Indian woman is meant to demurely stay within the household. That is Indian culture for them. How dare they go out at midnight to party like men? If they do that, they are meant to be criticised. This is the view of our custodians of culture. These are the same people who now pretend to be the protectors of our national symbols in the "New India". I fear we are moving towards a very dangerous brand of fascism.

January 19, 2017

PROTESTS OVER JALLIKATTU
HAVE NO BASE IN IDEOLOGY

"Trisha should be stripped naked and be chased on the road". This is just another abuse faced by Kollywood actor Trisha Krishnan, who left the shooting venue after an angry mob of Jallikattu supporters protested against her for endorsing PETA, People for the Ethical Treatment of Animals. A complete list of all these expletives can be found on Facebook that has been used against the actor.

What grave crime has Trisha committed to attract such an attack? Well... she just had a difference of opinion with regard to Jallikattu. For the record, Trisha has always projected herself as a serious animal rights activist, unlike her counterparts.

Apart from this, a few shooting units of Trisha's upcoming movies were also attacked by Jallikattu supporters. Following this the actor has retracted her earlier statements claiming to have not spoken anything against Jallikattu. Her mother has also approached the police, claiming her daughter's innocence and requested protection.

Following a ban on Jallikattu by the Supreme Court, there's a phenomenal rise in support for the sport across Tamil Nadu irrespective of the fact that Jallikattu is being conducted in merely four districts of the state. Also, it has been considered the pride of a particular caste group. The non-inclusion of dalits has also been a matter of contention over the years.

People who had no roots with Jallikattu have also joined the protest. A large number of students, with no political links, have been protesting. Around two lakh people have been protesting against the ban at Marina Beach. The media is unceasingly focusing on the protests and the film stars have also jumped in with their support to "save the pride of Tamils".

It would not be an exaggeration to say that Jallikattu protests are a massive people's rebellion after the anti-Hindi protests of 1965 in Tamil Nadu. But there's a vast difference between the two. The anti-Hindi agitation of 1965 had an ideological base, unlike the Jallikattu protest. This is nothing but a result of shock and anger in losing their racial identity, which has been crowning them for the last 1,000 years and that too by North Indians.

The Dravida Munnetra Kazhagam rose to power in Tamil Nadu simply by playing the Tamil identity card. After the early demise of C.N. Annadurai, the founder of DMK, his successor and five times chief minister M. Karunanidhi always pretended and ruled like a Chola king. The proof was the floral crown and the battle sword, which decorated him in all the meetings he was part of. After the rise of MGR, Mr Karunanidhi's dream of reigning was temporarily shattered. J. Jayalalitha went a step further by portraying herself as divine feminine form such as Mother Mary and Tamil goddess Mariyamma through thousands of cutouts.

In contemporary history, the LTTE's Prabhakaran was the proud symbol of Tamil ethnic identity. Many Tamil film directors are still claiming Prabhakaran as their leader, and this is the critical background with which the Jallikattu protest has to be viewed.

I have been approached by half a dozen TV channels a day for interviews regarding Jallikattu and I am continuously dismissing it. How can I?

My home is just a few minutes away from Marina Beach where people are protesting. What if some of them land up at my place? Who would protect my life?

This protest has been glorified and hailed by the media unanimously for their tremendous show of solidarity without any political leadership.

If mass unity is the matter of concern, I could cite the demolition of the Babri Masjid, which involved a unified crowd and mass solidarity. The former's mob fury was based on religious feelings and Jallikattu protests and connected rage is based on racial feelings. Not a vast difference, I guess.

The Jallikattu protest has taken a revolutionary mode due to media attention. The nature of the movement has been radically changed and the anger in minds of people against the governments in the state and Centre.

The protest against the Jallikattu ban is in no way connected to the earlier protests which the state has witnessed by several political parties; the demonstrations usually led to violent riots.

The scene at the Marina Beach was just like a "carnival". The air is filled with satisfying beats of folk dance and music being performed and street plays with strong messages to the Narendra Modi government. It was a blast!

Jallikattu is just a symbol. This student uprising is against corruption. And, lastly, I would like to point out that irrespective of the fact that the struggle is pointed towards Tamil identity, a major part of the youth cannot write in Tamil. Tamil is just a spoken language here, and that is an irony.

January 21, 2017

The highly-rated Netflix crime dramas Narcos and Breaking Bad would pale in comparison with the high-profile political drama being played out in the state of Tamil Nadu over the past few months. Former Tamil Nadu chief minister J. Jayalalitha fell sick, got admitted to Apollo Hospital late in the night and for the next couple of months there was no information on her illness or the treatment provided. The infamous "Mannargudi Mafia" which even disallowed the governor from meeting her, also managed to successfully hide her from the public eye. The media too was unable to access her or get any details about her treatment during the period. The Apollo press releases were equally evasive.

In a twist of events, Apollo one day suddenly announced that she had recovered fully and will be discharged any time, which was only followed by the news of her "sudden" death. There was utter confusion in even announcing the time of her death. The whole situation became a breeding ground for many conspiracy theories, one of which suggested that the former chief minister was dead long before the official announcement. None other than V.K. Sasikala directed this suspense thriller. And now she is stage-managing the ouster of the chief minister O. Panneerselvam.

Mr Panneerselvam, who had meekly tendered his resignation at her behest, finally gathered some courage after meditating at Jayalalitha's memorial and accused Chinnamma of hatching a conspiracy against him and forcing him to resign. His revolt has sent the social media in a tizzy with many hilarious memes doing the rounds: "Panneer should be thankful to Sasi for not sending him to Apollo".

Amidst all this drama a horrifying incident failed to grab the media's attention. On January 14, the decomposed body of a teenager with an underwear stuffed in her mouth was found in a well. The teen was identified as Nandini, a dalit from Ariyalur district in Tamil Nadu. This incident happened during the time when the Tamilians were searching for their identity through Jallikattu.

Nandini had quit school to work as a daily wage labourer in order to support her family. Manikandan, the local village Romeo, pursued her in true filmy style and managed to stay in a relationship with her for a year. Nandini soon became pregnant with his child and asked him to marry her. Manikandan refused and insisted on aborting the foetus, which led him along with his friends, to rape and murder the girl.

Although the culprits were arrested, the intermediate issues leading up to their arrest clearly exposed the casteist face of the crime. The police had repeatedly neglected requests by Nandini's mother to file an FIR, which was eventually done 17 days after her body was discovered. They even stooped to taunting Nandini's appearance and character. By refusing to lodge the complaint, the police gave time to the culprits. Manikandan belonged to upper caste and was also a functionary of a right-wing organisation, Hindu Munnani.

There was nationwide outrage over justice for Nirbhaya and the state of Tamil Nadu erupted over the murder of Swathi. But sadly nobody spoke for Nandini, the dalit.

The wells of Ariyalur have a past of witnessing the murder of four dalit children on May 5, 1980, when an upper caste maniac electrocuted them. When it comes to man-woman relationships, Indian society can be accused of outdated morals. The regressive nature of most television debates proves that this country is still stuck in the Middle Ages. On top of this, Ramagopalan, the founder-leader of HM, claimed that the girl had mutilated her genitals with a blade!

Nandini's brutal murder and society's reaction to it exposes its caste bias. P.S. A special thanks to Vincent Kathir of Evidence for the fieldwork he has undertaken to unearth the realities behind the rape and murder of Nandini.

February 12, 2017

FILM

THE JOY AND PAIN OF GOOD
CINEMA

Once, during an interview, I was asked, "What fascinates you more than your writing?" I replied instantly, "Wine, women and God," forgetting to add the fourth thing that enthralls me: cinema. During my Delhi years with the rationing department, from 1978 to 1990, Rangayan theatre was the place to watch cinema. Being a steno, I used to visit every juggi-jhopri with my boss to issue ration cards.

The then lieutenant-governor of Delhi, Jagmohan, probably impressed by my "field work", invited me to join his staff. I thought about the offer, and politely declined.

The rationing department was located in the Civil Lines area of Old Delhi where the Indraprastha College for Women was also located. (When recollecting locations, only attractive landmarks, like the IP College for Women, remain etched in the memory, doesn't it?) One Chandan Singh, with a bushy "Nietzsche" moustache, ran a tea shop near the college. Some other eatables also were available at his stall. But every day for me it was toasted bread and chhole for breakfast. Never in my life have I savoured such delicious chhole anywhere else.

I never got a chance to really visit Delhi after 1990, except a couple of times for a few days at the India International Centre to attend literary meets. Delhi is the place where my literary life began. If I were asked about my native place, I would rather talk about Delhi than the place I was born and grew up in. I was familiar with every street, nook and corner of Delhi.

In those 12 years, learning Hindi was the most unforgettable of all my experiences. My Hindi vocabulary could not have exceeded a dozen words when I set foot in Delhi. On the first day a colleague said to me, "Hey Madrasi babu, ek kagaz do"; I disliked being addressed as "Madrasi". (Even today, if someone introduces me as a "Tamil writer", I feel squeamish. Can you imagine someone introducing Paulo Coelho as a Portuguese writer or Umberto Eco as an Italian writer?) To escape this Madrasi identity meant mingling with my civil supplies colleagues and shedding the "Madrasi accent". All this stuff I learnt later on, but on the first day I did not even know what kagaz was till my friend waved a sheet of paper.

That very day I started learning Hindi from the chaprasis. The quandary was that my Hindi got enriched with too many cuss words. I never managed to speak Hindi without uttering "behen...", "maa...", which received delighted encouragement from my Punjabi friends.

I journeyed north last year, for the sole reason of seeing my beloved Delhi. First thing I did was to visit Chandan Singh's dukan. Good old Chandan Singh welcomed me with tea. Was it sweeter than what it used to be? No. The quantum of sugar remained unchanged in 21 years, though I have arrived at the "cheeni kum" age.

All these memories started flooding me while I was

watching *Gangs of Wasseypur* recently. In the Eighties, there were no computers and no DVDs. I could watch films only at the Delhi Film Society or in embassies. I used to ramble from embassy to embassy, chasing films. In fact, the very first book I wrote was about Latin American cinema. In that book I wrote elaborately about less-known directors then, like Jorge Sanjines, Glauber Rocha etc. So far I have written six books on international, Hindi and Tamil cinemas (all in Tamil, of course).

I recall watching *Dev D*. It sent shivers down my spine, like it would have done to every Indian who, like me, had been obsessively following cinema. Then on I started watching Hindi films with a keen interest, especially films by Anurag Kashyap. I wrote in detail about *Dev D*, under the title "The Madness of Lust and the Pinnacle of Art". The synopsis is this: *Dev D* subverted and demolished pseudo-simplicity and traditions considered sacrosanct in all the aspects of filmmaking — story, dialogue, editing, music, cinematography (for example, you can compare Italian designer Ettore Sotsass' psychedelics with *Dev D*'s cinematography, particularly the song *Emotional Atyachaar*). I regard it as the first post-modern film from Bollywood.

After Dev D, followed *Gulaal* — and then onwards you could say that I became a dedicated fan of the Mumbai triumvirate — Anurag Kashyap, Amit Trivedi and Piyush Mishra. On the same note, films like Dibakar Banerjee's *Love, Sex aur Dhoka*, Onir's *I Am*, Vishal Bharadwaj's *7 Khoon Maaf* and now Kashyap's *Gangs of Wasseypur* have demolished the established norms of serious cinema tradition. They have dropped the "Bollywood trash" tag by exploiting the very same genre, and transforming it into subversive cinema.

In Tamil art cinema — assuming that the absence of songs, dance, comedy, action etc. means serious cinema — they roll out films that not a single soul manages to watch fully and get out alive. Few optimistic audiences take a tea break hoping that things will change on re-entry, but are totally bewildered to see that the famished, torn and battered hero (the hero actually survived on meagre meals for a few days before the shoot — See, it is realism!) searching for food for half an hour in the trash can. This is what intellectuals here celebrate as good cinema. (The only exception recently has been *Aaranya Kaandam*. It is a real classic and the best film ever made in Tamil Nadu. But it was a flop and Kollywood has driven director Thiagarajan Kumararaja to Mumbai, on the pretext that his film is decadent.)

Gangs of Wasseypur contains 14 songs and the composer is Sneha Khanwalkar. After Piyush Mishra and Amit Trivedi, she has become one of my favourite composers. Listening to the song *Bhoos*, sung by the prisoners, I kept thinking how rare it is to listen to such original folk music in Indian cinema. The voices and music in this film's songs challenge the traditional models. How can one describe the feelings of euphoria and celebration after listening to the song *Jiya Tu* played after the film's hero, Sardar Khan, is shot dead?

So far I have written reviews of numerous films, but felt *Gangs of Wasseypur* was beyond comprehension. Can you describe in words your most wonderful sexual experience?

July 8, 2012

KAMMATTIPAADAM: WELCOME TO DALIT NOIR AND IT IS BRILLIANT

"From worms to tigers, from insects to eagles, from elephant seals to all other creatures of wild; and different Gods from different times along with us the Polayars lead a wretched life, we all struggle alike and die in this world, my beloved son."

'*Kammattipaadam*' starts with this lovely song.

Krishnan (Dulquer Salmaan) who works as a security guard in Mumbai gets a telephone call from his childhood friend Ganga. The call drops. Realising that his friend is in trouble, Krishnan leaves at once for Kammattipaadam, his native place. From there on, it's a three-hour flashback which takes us to Kammattipaadam, a slum in Ernakulam. It's the 1970s. Ganga's elder brother Balan is a small time hooch smuggler and a henchman. Friends Ganga and Krishnan grow up in the shadow of Balan the rowdy, and join him in the trade. Once when Krishnan and Ganga are smuggling spirit, they are confronted by the police. In a bid to save his friend, Krishnan accidentally kills a policeman and is sent to jail.

Meantime, the residents of Kammattipaadam are being forcibly, illegally cleared out to build an apartment complex. Balan, who was initially supportive of the mafia don who forcefully evacuated the slum dwellers, now wants to lead a more sedate life that doesn't bring him in conflict with law. Before he could embark on a reformed life, his enemies kill him.

At a young age, Krishnan and Anita, a relative of Ganga, fall in love. Their romance is picturised very realistically, which is quite a departure from the over-the-topness of Indian cinematic tradition. Ganga holds Krishnan indirectly responsible for his brother's death. And, he marries Krishnan's love interest Anita.

'*Kammattipaadam*' grasps the plight of the marginalized - in this case, the Pulayars, comprising the bottom of the barrel even among Dalits - with astonishing accuracy. That alone makes it a must-watch.

o

Kammattipaadam is an authentic Charu Nivedita biopic I did not script. The young Krishnan is me, almost. Like the Pulayars of this film there were Thombars - a Telugu-speaking community of manual scavengers - in my village in Tamil Nadu. In the social pecking order, the Kattu Naickan family (another Telugu-speaking tribe) I was born in, was only marginally, 'higher' than the Thombars. Our community's stock-in-trade, according to tradition, was hunting. But due to deforestation and urbanization, we resorted to smuggling and thieving. If the police got us, they'd tie our legs together and rain bamboo stick-blows like horseshoes hammered into equine hooves. Our folk were raised on a regular diet of oxtail soup, known for its pain-numbing powers.

In one violent attempt at looting a house in broad

daylight, I was caught by the police. There were witnesses to nail me for good. The local police inspector was a decent chap. He called me home. The fact that I was the best student in my class may have helped. But I suspect I earned his sympathy because my skin was fairer than others of my ilk. 'Once a case is filed against you, you'll remain a criminal for the rest of your life. Finish your final year at school and scoot from this place,' he helpfully said. I haven't been to my Kammattipaadam since.

Mindless violence, fuelled by alcoholism is part of everyday life for dalits in rural India, and most urban shanties. No Indian film has portrayed this as powerfully as *Kammattipaadam*. Besides a few in Kannada, no south Indian film has captured the dalit life in such great detail or nuance. In Tamil, director Selvaraghavan's 'Pudhupettai', or Pa. Ranjith's 'Madras' capture the lives of the marginalized somewhat authentically, but they eventually fall prey to *masala* temptations. It can safely be argued that *Kammattipaadam*, moving away from the mainstream, has introduced to us a brand new dalit cinematic aesthetic.

Now to the niggles. One, the climax succumbs to Indian filmy trope of revenge. Two, Dulquer Salmaan is an utter disappointment. His acting is as constipated as former Tamil hero Ramarajan's (he of the AIADMK-coloured, red-white-black shirts and orange lipstick fame).

Vinayakan (Ganga) and Manikandan (Balan), can teach Dulquer Salmaan an acting lesson or two.

This film reminds me of Oscar Lewis' 1966 book *La*

Vida which analyses the state people living in Puerto Rico's slums. Lewis through his book advanced the idea that big-money anti-poverty schemes would come a cropper if education was not at the foundation of it all.

India's villages and urban slums remain Kammattipaadams because our policymakers and politicians have not understood this culture of poverty. Instead, they choose to rain freebies such as television sets, and mobile phones.

One cannot praise enough director Rajeev Ravi's courage for telling us, unapologetically, the stories of people whose lives are no different from that of slaughter animals we rear in claustrophobic pens. *Kammattipaadam* is the hardest slap of realism on our face in recent times.

June 4, 2016

* * *

IRAIVI TAMIL MOVIE REVIEW: MAKING A CASE FOR CASUAL IMMORALITY

I watched *Iraivi* (Goddess) on the very day of its release, last Friday because director Karthik Subbaraj's previous effort *Jigarthanda* was a differently made commercial film. In a nutshell, I felt like I was thrown into a sewer with my hands and feet firmly tied. We could quietly let this pass if it were merely a bad film. *Iraivi* is a testament to Tamil Nadu's cultural debasement.

Director-turned-actor S.J. Surya (don't ask me his name in the film; my mind went so numb that it didn't register) plays a film director. For some reason, the theatrical release of his new film - a great, great Bergman-beating, Kurosawa-trumping piece of artistic work, we are repeatedly told - is stuck. His spirits broken, Surya hits the bottle big time. And that is an understatement. He drinks from six in the evening till six in the morning. There is not a moment when he doesn't drink. Surya's brother, played by Bobby Simha and Vijay Sethupathi, join him, and they all drink some more. The three smoke so much that they could, by themselves, deplete the whole of the ozone layer. What they speak makes absolutely no sense.

Surya has a six-or-seven-year-old daughter. When she leaves for school, he staggers home from the bar. 'If this continues, I'll divorce you soon,' says his wife in mild disapproval of his conduct. But like the Nalayini of our epic, she understands her husband's pain that has led him to alcohol. I fully expected the wife, Nalayini-like, to carry Surya in a basket to the brothel. But no. Surya was too good a man. He only drinks because his 'world's best' film isn't being let out of the tin.

His friend, Vijay Sethupathi has a love interest. But the girl, who is the harbourer of 'revolutionary' views does not care much for love and matters of the heart. That sex alone forms the basis of a man-woman relationship, is her unshakeable belief. However, for all her radicalism on the matter, she shies away from using the S-word. Throughout the film, she refers to it as the 'three-letter-word'. Vijay Sethupathi pesters the 'radical chick' to marry him. She keeps chanting the 'three-letter' mantra. Exasperated, he asks his parents to find a girl for him. Is this the 1960s, I wonder. Haven't they thought about these so called 'live-in' relationships? But I forget, the act of thinking, or thought, has nothing to do do with this film. Vijay Sethupathi eventually gets married to Anjali. He lights a cigarette during their first night together. The girl asks, 'Oh you smoke.' 'Don't ask such questions because I haven't married you out of choice,' he says and goes to sleep alone. Are these people from Planet Nova?

Meantime, the great director Surya's wife and father approach the producer of the greatest film to resolve the release tangle. The producer asks for Rs six crore to get the movie out. The whole family - father, brothers, friend - huddles together in a hospital (they are there because

Surya's mother has been in coma for a very long time) to arrive at a solution. Just as he shouts in a drunken rage throughout the film, Surya does that in the hospital as well. A disapproving nurse arrives. Surya shouts after she leaves. Then she returns. Surya shouts again. This is getting tedious, right? I wanted to leave the theatre within 10 minutes of the film's start. Sadly, I had the last seat, and exiting would mean stepping on the toes of 15 people in the darkness. Therefore, I waited for the intermission.

To get the six crore rupees, Bobby Simha's grand plan is to steal an antique statue of a goddess. Surya initially disapproves. Bobby says, he's done it in the past. 'No risk,' he adds sunnily. At the end of the discussion, even Surya's father (played by Radha Ravi) gives the green light for the planned heist. As justification, he argues, 'to get one work of art out in the midst of people, stealing another is no crime.' What profound philosophy! They talk of stealing national treasure as if it were akin to buying a packet of cigarettes. The problem with *Iraivi* is not that it is a bad film, but that it advances, and glorifies ideas that are downright dangerous for the society. I'm pretty certain youngsters who watch the film would think that it is okay to steal if you are in a tight spot; it's okay to turn into an alcoholic if there's trouble at work. Like displays of casual racism in our films, this is propagation of casual immorality.

In countless interviews, Karthik Subbaraj, the film's director, claimed that 'Iraivi' glorified women. Upon closer examination, what he probably means is that the character of Anjali (who marries Sethupathy) is modelled on Damayanti, or Nalayini. Anjali gets pregnant. Sethupathy seeks out his former lover. 'Hey, what is the bottom line?' he asks. The girl continues to bang on about the 'three-letter' word but asks him if he hasn't touched his wife. At that precise moment, a young man walks into her house. 'Who's that?' queries Sethupathy. 'Take a guess,' says the girl. Our friend storms out. Just then, the new entrant hands a laptop to her and says, 'I have made it all right, sister.' He repeats the word sister twice. Then comes the scene that according to the director is the apogee of cinematic depiction of feminism. Looking at Sethupathy from the window, the girl who believed only in the 'three-letter' word, sobs uncontrollably.

Imagine a lunatic asylum whose inmates have been fed six pegs of cheap brandy. The result would resemble *Iraivi*.

June 5, 2016

UDTA PUNJAB : CAUGHT BETWEEN SOCIAL MESSAGE AND *MASALA*

Since our esteemed censor board had recommended no fewer than 94 cuts for *Udta Punjab*, my decision to watch the film had turned into an immovable object. If a film has ruffled so many of the censor board feathers, chances usually are that it would be good. Another reason why I wanted to watch it was Anurag Kashyap who happens to be one of *Udta Punjab*'s producers. Any film Kashyap is associated with, I am more often than not, the first in line at the theatres. The film's opening scenes fully vindicated my rule of thumb.

Pinky is a hockey player from Bihar. Poverty pushes her upland to Punjab to work as a farm labourer. A stash of heroin worth a crore, accidentally lands in her lap. It took me a while to recognize that it was Alia Bhatt playing Pinky. Her makeup (or the complete lack of it) that made her look every bit like a village girl, was utterly authentic. Pinky thinks she could sell the contents of the accidentally - procured bag for a few thousand rupees. There begins her misery. The owners of the heroin package start a hunt for Pinky. She throws it in a well. Captured, she is raped, repeatedly.

Addicted-to-drugs rockstar Tommy a.k.a Gabru's (Shahid Kapoor) young fans are also in the habit of substance abuse. Among them is a schoolboy called Balli. His elder brother is an Assistant Sub-inspector of police, Sartaj (Diljit Dosanjh). Preet (Kareena Kapoor) works as a doctor at a drug rehabilitation centre in Punjab. The story of these characters is braided into one by director Abhishek Chaubey, to tell a tale of drug-infested Punjab.

Generally, films that desperately try to carry a social message end up being more messed up than even hardcore *masala* entertainers. In Tamil, directors Bala and Vasantha Balan manage to give me this experience unfailingly. Since they are worshipped as demi-gods in the state, I have earned a million enemies for being critical of their work. But we digress. However, the alternative cinema produced by Bollywood can often hold a candle to world cinema. Therefore, I had high hopes from *Udta Punjab*.

There is so much sermonizing in the movie that after 30 minutes of runtime, the film resembled a DAVP anti-drug abuse campaign. It felt like I was thrust into a moral science lecture at high school. Between 1978 and 1990, when I worked for the Central Civil Supplies Department, I was posted at Delhi. By and large, Madrasi Central Government employees in Delhi would find a way to end up in the south Block. They would find residence in the south Indian ghettos of R.K. Puram or Munirka. My office happened to be in northern Delhi. I lived in Punjabi Bagh, both pretty large Punjabi settlements. During that period, I had also travelled extensively across Punjab. Hailing from a state where vivacity was an alien concept that was scoffed at, I spent those 12 years in a bit of a culture shock. No matter the magnitude of the problem facing them, the Punjabis that I knew were an irrepressible lot who epitomized the *khao, piyo, aish karo* (eat, drink and be merry) zeitgeist. How the youth from a such a land came into the evil embrace of narcotics, is something *Udta Punjab* stubbornly refuses to probe. The director deals with the origins of the malaise in the most superficial manner. Moreover, every 10 minutes or so, there comes a heavy dose of anti-drug sermon, giving one the unmistakable feeling of sitting through a documentary. If an unsparing editor had pruned the film shorter by 45 minutes, *Udta Punjab* would be more gripping.

In the last 60 minutes, the film suddenly takes a turn towards the mundane-*masala* territory. Shahid Kapoor embarks on a mission to save the heroine on a bicycle. A close-up of the milestone shows the destination to be 108 kilometres away. Forget a drug-addict, even those who train diligently every morning for months to participate in their city's half-marathon would find it difficult to pedal for 108 kilometres overnight, non-stop, at a steady pace of 10 kms/hour. In every commercial film, at the apex of any cross-border drug racket, there has to be a politician. *Udta Punjab* faithfully follows that template.

Despite the overall flatness, the film manages a few highs. Chief among them is Amit Trivedi's music. In the first song Chitta ve, Trivedi fuses Punjabi words with electronica in a fabulous fashion. The Diljit Dosanjh version of *Ik kudi* is soul-stirring. The background music, in keeping with the theme, is suitably psychedelic. I was sold on Trivedi's music since *Dev D*. But this film hardly does justice to the magnificence of his music. I returned home and while listening to the songs on YouTube, found myself in a state of trance.

The other massive plus for the film is Alia Bhatt's acting. I cannot find the words to praise her enough, nor any other performance in recent times to match it. The dialogues throughout the film are dazzling. In every scene, Sudip Sharma, the writer, brings out the essence of rural Punjab. When the rock star introduces himself to Pinky as Tommy, "Are you a dog?" she asks him!

The key shortcoming of this film compared to *Dev D* or *Queen* is its lack of intensity. The storyline too is not quite strong. It starts with the grave societal problem of drug-abuse and ends with the hero rescuing the heroine from dastardly villains. The intellectuals, however, have gone all sentimental about this film, shedding copious tears in their reviews.

It is probably proof that it is easier to make the intellectuals cry than common folk!

June 18, 2016

RAMAN RAGHAV 2.0 REVEALS OUR DEMONIC HALF

When friends asked me how *Raman Raghav 2.0* was, I was irritated. Can one ask, 'How was the movie?' for a film directed by Christopher Nolan, Quentin Tarantino or Alejandro González Iñárritu? Similarly, Anurag Kashyap's *Raman Raghav 2.0* is an experience. A superb artistic experience.

A single scene, which I consider one of the best I have seen in my world cinema experience, illustrates this: Raman has just escaped from police custody and arrives to meet his sister. She is terrified of him, fearing that he will destroy her serene middle-class life. Her husband disrespects Raman, who would never tolerate such an insult. What follows is a 'theatre of cruelty'. Raman ties up his brother-in-law and nephew and sends his sister to buy chicken. It has been four days since he last ate, he claims, since he was not fed in the 'secret' police custody. The sister purchases the meat, unable to inform anyone at the market about what is happening at home. Holding the lives of his sister, her husband and their child in his iron rod, Raman cooks and eats the chicken. The scene is stunning.

Words fail me when I try to describe how fantastic Nawazuddin Siddiqui's acting was. But the clincher for Raman is that there is no motive to any of his killings.

Usually, cinematic serial killers are shown to have an awful childhood as some justification for their crimes. There is no such back-story here. Raman kills his victims as casually as if he were having a cup of tea.

The other protagonist in the movie is Assistant Commissioner of police, Raghav (Vicky Kaushal), who is on a mission to catch Raman. Raghav is a drug addict. While there is no back story as to why Raman became a serial killer, there is one for Raghav. Raghav's girlfriend, Simmy (played by a voluptuous Sobhita Dhulipala), is an intense character. Her relationship with Raghav is no greater than the relationship between Raman and his victims. Ignoring Simmy, he brings home girls and makes love to them. Being a drug addict, he is unable to perform in bed. Even Viagra does not help. He lives a life full of violence, despair and anxiety. (None of these are found in Raman.) Despite all this, Simmy loves him truly.

"Suggested or stimulated by reflections in mirrors and water and by twins, the idea of the Double is common to many countries. It is likely that sentences such as 'A friend is another self' by Pythagoras, or the Platonic 'Know thyself' were inspired by it," are the opening lines of Jorge Luis Borges' *The Double*. Ever since childhood, we are prescribed do's and don'ts and the don'ts pile up day after day. Am I Raman or Raghav? Godse or Gandhi? This Borgesian question is the motif of Raman Raghav.

Whenever a crime happens, people think that a criminal is a man sent from hell, and we act as though we are very kind human beings; or we believe we are so. But we too are responsible for that crime. The criminal is no different from us. Our only solace is that we are not in his situation. Had we been there, we would be committing that act of crime. This point is emphasized strongly by the film's shooting spots. The film is shot exquisitely in slums, which are uninhabitable by humans. These locations constantly remind us that we could be Raman if we were born in those slums. Newborns are kidnapped in India every other month. They are made to beg at traffic signals. Sometimes, their heart and kidneys are stolen. One cannot imagine how violent these kids can be. A 10-year-old kid, bred in such a situation, can commit any crime. Sexual crimes are only a matter for two years later. We are lucky to not be in this situation.

The gruesome murders in the films of directors like Michael Haneke, metamorphose into art in the hands of Anurag Kashyap. First-rate cinematography and music greatly assist this magic. The music (Ram Sampath) is in sync with the mood of the film, but being an Amit Trivedi addict, I missed him greatly.

June 26, 2016

* * *

OZHIVU DIVASATHE KALI: THIS 20 LAKH MALAYALAM FILM IS AMONG INDIA'S FINEST EVER

The Malayalam film *Ozhivu Divasathe Kali* (Holiday Revelry), directed by Sanal Kumar Sasidharan has changed many of my long-held perceptions about cinema. Especially about the finance involved in the making of films. In Tamil, we are talking sums of around 20 crore even for alternate cinema. That is because even the music directors' salaries run into crores irrespective of the nature of the film.

There is no background score in Ozhivu *Divasathe Kali,* only naturally occurring ambient sounds. The sound of rain, the songs of birds. Just as our real lives chug along without background music. But that hardly hampers the plot's grip over the viewer. *Ozhivu Divasathe Kali* was made on an astoundingly tiny budget of ⌧20 lakh. Yes, 20 lakh. When I learnt that Raman Raghav cost 3.5 crore to film, it took me some time to emerge from the depths of disbelief. *Ozhivu Divasathe Kali* with its piffling production cost is nothing short of a revolution in Indian cinema. Usually, films made on such shoe-string budgets fall woefully short on aesthetic parameters. Every scene would reek of the filmmaker's poverty. But *Ozhivu Divasathe Kali* bucks that trend. It feels like a magnificent Krzysztof Kieślowski film rather than one made with basement bargain budgets.

It's next accomplishment, the story. Five friends, during

their election-time vacation, decide to go to the forest. In no time, the small supply of alcohol they've taken along, is exhausted. There is talk, talk and more talk. It rains endlessly as it indeed does in the forests of Kerala. The torrent of talk and rain is unrelenting. Since the events unfold in the midst of polling, there is election-related news playing constantly in the background. A middle-aged woman agrees to cook some chicken for the holidaymakers. Nothing else happens. Our cinematic instinct expects the woman to be raped, gang raped, killed, or just that she would trigger something dramatic. None of that happens.

Chicken curry would be the ideal accompaniment for alcohol in the forest. The woman says she can cook but will not kill the bird herself. The men too are reluctant. The task is eventually entrusted to one of the five friends. Even he finds the act of beheading the bird with his bare hands too gruesome. He hangs it by the neck on a tree to meet a slow, unaided death.

Some in the group eye the woman lasciviously. They hope the fruit might plop into their lap. Intimidated by her glare that is good enough to burn wet wood, one man in the gang drops out. Another more persistent member loses his will upon seeing her wield the knife. She finishes cooking, collects her fee and disappears. Intermission.

With the woman--on whom rested our expectations of thrilling twists and turns--gone, the film is now sustained only by the bacchanalia of the friends. With their liquor ration running out, one of them is dispatched to a nearby town which is three to four kilometres away, to procure more. Since it is polling day, the black market is his only option. Somehow, he manages to return with a full bottle. Drinking resumes, so does the chatter. I shan't tell you of the incident which is the film's climax. Take my car, go watch it.

If someone narrated such a story to Tamil film directors, chances are they'd be brutally beaten up.

How the director could produce a work of utter genius with the one-line plot of how-five-friends-drink-themselves-silly-in-the-forest is mindboggling.

Make no mistake, *Ozhivu Divasathe Kali* is a classic. This is where we need to talk a bit about literature. In what ways can cinema use literature? Ozhivu Divasathe Kali is based on Malayalam writer Unni R's short story. To adapt such a short story, the maker needs a quality that goes beyond understanding cinema and literature. That quality is called wisdom--a wisdom that is gained from arts such as literature, cinema, music or dance. When literature accumulates in us only in the form of information, it is merely knowledge.

Ozhivu Divasathe Kali's two prominent themes are Women and Dalit politics. There are countless films that tackle these two themes. However, *Ozhivu Divasathe Kali* is far removed from the films that you can think of.

One of the friends continually stares at the woman's ample hips. In those fleeting scenes, the woman is perceived as an object of desire, like alcohol or the chicken meat that the men crave. The man with the hip fetish follows her and tries to make contact. He steps back when she brandishes her giant knife. Another man tries to chat her up.

'How many kids?'

'One.'

'Which grade?'

'Tenth.'

'Oh, tenth? You don't look like the mother of such an old girl.'

She does not even acknowledge his words. Repudiated, the man steps aside.

Women figure prominently during the drinking sessions. 'Sex is fine if the woman consents. To use force is rape,' argues one. 'How's that? Isn't man always on top?' demurs another.

'Which means you've only been raping your wife all along.'

'How dare you drag my wife into this?' And then ensues a brawl. Two friends meditate; they drink some more.

Punctuated by a series of such arguments, their marathon drinking session continues. When one such discussion gets too hot, one miffed member of the group decides to walk away. The scene where he's pacified lasts about 10-15 minutes. It is all Pinteresque theatre of the absurd.

Ozhivu Divasathe Kali is a must watch for students of filmmaking as well as superstar directors who do not make films under 100 crore. This 106-minute film has been filmed in about 70 shots while the trend in mainstream commercial cinema is to have several thousands. Many shots in the film range from 5 to 20 minutes. The 53 minutes after the intermission is a single shot. Generally, films that employ this technique exasperate the viewer. On the contrary, *Ozhivu Divasathe Kali* only heightens our expectations.

For all this, the film neither has a written-down script nor a screenplay. The dialogues were written at the shooting location. That was made possible because of the story and the politics in the story. The killing of the chicken is the film's primary motif. Post interval, the drunken conversations attain an altogether ethereal plane.

Ozhivu Divasathe Kali can only be described as a miracle product of Indian cinema.

July 18, 2016

* * *

KABALI AND THE MASS HYSTERIA
OF TAMILS

In the olden days, a huddle of touts and black-marketers could be seen outside cinema halls. During the first few days of a big release, the halls would turn into a fiefdom of black ticket sellers. Nowadays, corporate companies are doing that job with great élan. Black marketing is a crime in India. But in India, it is a crime only when committed by the lumpen. When large corporate firms do it, it becomes the accepted practice.

Sample this recent Facebook post by a friend: "For the last one week I've made the rounds of every theatre in the city, morning and evening, that's screening Kabali. There are hundreds of people at all times hoping to get their hands on one ticket. They hang around there listening to every invective in the Tamil dictionary from the security guard.

The reality is that all tickets for Kabali have been shared around among corporates, VVIPs and VIPs. The hoi polloi can get a look in only after the third day. One Chennai theatre is charging Rs 5,000 for an unofficial 12.50 am screening of the film. In the same movie hall, the tickets for official screening cost Rs 1,000."

Not only are software firms in Chennai hoarding tickets, but they've also declared an official holiday on the day of Kabali's launch.

The producer of the film, S. Thanu, got a favourable judgment from the Madras High Court which restrained the license of 169 registered Internet Service Providers (ISPs) in India from permitting illegal downloads of Kabali. By the same token shouldn't there be some regulation on the movie makers' extortionist pricing tactics?

But that hasn't dampened the desire of eight crore Tamils to watch Kabali on 'Day One'. The whole state is in the grips of a mass hysteria. In everyday Tamil life, there is no recreational avenue other than films. A Rajini film, therefore, is the apogee of entertainment. The hysteria that Rajini releases whip up is a result of the herd mentality that we witness during New Year's Eve in other Indian cities. Sometimes this hysteria manifests itself when celebrities die. Since we are utterly bereft of heroes to look up to, we end up creating icons and start worshipping them.

People in Tamil Nadu, by and large, shy away from critiquing this Kabali-related hysteria. One of the key distributors and exhibitors of the film in Tamil Nadu is close to the powers that are in the ruling party. The television rights for Kabali have been lapped up by Jaya TV. When the DMK was in power, things were very much the same. Karunanidhi's family virtually controlled every bit of the state's entertainment industry. The Sun TV group were a part of the consortium that produced the previous Rajini superhit, *Endhiran.*

This mass hysteria would have been tempered if people even had a passing acquaintance with literature or world cinema. A Bergman film may not be everyone's cup of tea, but if an entire society turns philistine with a vengeance, Rajini-mania is what we will end up with.

July 21, 2016

KABALI IS NEITHER A RAJINI
FILM NOR A RANJITH FILM

Pa Ranjith's previous directorial efforts, *Madras* and *Attakathi*, were a bit different from the standard *masala* fare of Tamil cinema. Kollywood buzz had it that Rajinikanth, the emperor of *masala* corn, zeroed in on Ranjith for *Kabali* to break the mould.

The hype around the film was so much that even taxi drivers earning 20,000 a month were willing to spend ₹3,000 on a first day, first show ticket for *Kabali*. For such people, this kind of splurge is a hot sponge that temporarily alleviates the pain of their tedious, monotonous lives. In Bolivia, people are known to chew on cocoa leaves to kill hunger pangs. The Chinese in the previous century used opium for the same purpose. It seems the Tamils--rich and poor--seek a brief relief from their humdrum existence in Rajinikanth films.

In the face of unprecedented demand, I somehow managed to wangle a ticket for Kabali on the day of its release.

The film and the entire experience of *Kabali* were pitiable.

Here's a small sampling of the things I felt sorry for:

1. The audience: Families came in droves as if this was

the biggest day of celebration in their lives. They wore *Kabali* T-shirts with great pride.

2. Rajinikanth: A disclaimer at the very beginning said no animals were harmed in the making of the film. Excellent. But is it alright to harm the elderly in the process of making the movie? Here, I mean Rajinikanth. He is only 66. But in the film, he looks like he is 86.

He appears rather tired and exhausted throughout the film. No amount of makeup could correct the discernible sag in his physical appearance. Why put an old man through so much torture? Can he not play roles which commensurate with his vintage? Even though he, for the bulk of the film, portrays the role of a 60-year-old man, he is called upon to enact action sequences like he did more than 20 years ago in *Batsha.*

Think of the wonderful Amitabh Bachchan film, *The Last Lear,* directed by Rituparno Ghosh. In the film, he plays the role of a 70-year-old stage actor. Bachchan has not given a finer performance. The Last Lear is one of the most memorable films I have seen.

What prevents Rajinikanth from picking such roles? Rajinikanth is potentially a better actor than his contemporary Kamal Haasan. It is the blighted image trap. Instead of making dross of the Kabali variety and deceiving himself and the audience in the process, Rajini must break out of the image trap if he wishes to prolong his career.

3. Director Pa Ranjith: He is the most pitiable of the lot. He is one of the most talented young directors in Tamil

cinema today. Young directors such as Ranjith should not be entangled with superstars. In *Kabali*, there is not a trace of Ranjith. There were moments in the film when the fans seemed positively apoplectic, not knowing how to react.

Out of the blue, just as *Kabali* readies to kill the baddie, he launches into a monologue. It was as if Karl Marx had come out of the grave and started incoherently reading from Das Kapital. At that point, I closed my eyes tight and prayed to God to save me from this farce.

There isn't one thrilling sequence in the film. It was like watching a television soap.

The scene that takes the biscuit in boredom is when Kabali has a conversation with kids of the rehabilitation centre that he runs. It reminded me of times when village schools would conduct moral science classes at two in the afternoon where both the teachers and students would doze off. This is not a Ranjith film. This is a film made for Rajinikanth. But then, how can a 66-year-old perform the histrionics that even a 26-year-old cannot? As a result, Kabali ends up as neither a Rajini film nor a Ranjith film.

Putting his career at stake, Ranjith has sent a valuable message to fellow young directors, that they should shun superstars. If they make films with superstars, they will not bear the director's signature because actors continue to call the shots.

There may be a few directors such as Mani Ratnam, Mysskin and Bala who make the films they want to. But it is an extremely small club.

July 23, 2016

INTERVIEWS

"He writes in bold face"

Hay Session: 'A Song of Celebration, A Song of Freedom'

Reporting by Shradha. S for Yentha, November 13, 2010.

In session with Rakesh Khanna, the Tamil writer Charu Nivedita has some harsh words for the double standards that prevail in modern Indian society, more specifically in Tamil Nadu. He has been writing in Tamil, English and Malayalam, for the past 30 years with almost 45 published works till date.

In his land, Tamil Nadu, Charu Nivedita is almost anonymous. It is this anonymity that keeps him safe in spite of his provoking writings and explicit content that are almost never published in his home-state. The bureaucrats remain ignorant of his existence though he and his contemporaries have a hardcore readership, be it columns or personal blogs.

In contrast, "Kerala has adopted me as their own writer." The fact that he has his own column in leading Malayalam dailies on world music, film reviews and criticisms attests to it.

He is a 'voracious' reader of Tamil literature, and thinks that a majority of the contemporary writings are unnoticed because of the Westerner's craze towards the 2,000 Sangam literature, misunderstood as the sole representation of Tamil literary scene. "We have poets more powerful than Pablo Neruda and they are un-recognized. Tamil writers of today are treated as folk artists and mediocre ones are given importance," says he.

On his reception among critics, he says: "My writings are labeled vulgar, though they just represent what happens around us, that makes people think that I am a porn-writer, which I am not."

Nietzsche is his 'master' and his works are a celebration of life.

He thinks it is extremely lamentable that writers today reject each other and fight to get better readership and commercial value. He points out: "While Latin American countries either celebrate their writers or make them ambassadors or kill them, in our land they are not even given recognition."

To him, the web is an easier space to write without much investment, unlike the early days of having to get your works published, and at times going to the extent of pledging your personal belongings to finance your work.

He thinks the biggest failures of our society are the pseudo intellects and the kind of followers they get. On a scandalous note he winds up saying, "I am not averse to anyone. I just want to prevent the dangerous things they are doing to the language."

The session also saw an interesting reading of excerpts in Tamil from his book 'Zero Degree' and the translated versions by Rakesh Khanna and Kaveri, much to the delight of the audience.

* * *

MY NOVEL WAS TREATED LIKE A SONG OF FREEDOM

———

Interviewed by Faizal Khan

The Economic Times

November 18, 2010

When a publisher of cheap detective novels in Tamil asked Charu Nivedita if he agreed with him for a cover price of ten rupees for his new novel, the writer didn't flinch. "Please go ahead and print it," he concurred. The result was a book in newsprint that had a print run of 50,000 copies.

"It was bad printing," says Nivedita, who had sold his wife's mangal sutra to publish the same novel on his own two years earlier, but without much success. The cheap edition of Zero Degree came as a blessing in disguise. Not only did it help Charu achieve a huge readership among the masses, it led to better-published translations, first in Malayalam, and now in English.

At about the same time, California-born Rakesh Khanna was having his evening tea at a roadside tea stall in Chennai when he saw an advertisement of a ten-rupee novel in a local magazine. "I got curious and first found the book and later its author," says Khanna, who runs the Blaft Publications in Chennai. In 2008, Khanna published the first translation of Zero Degree in English.

On the opening day of the Hay literary festival in Thiruvananthapuram, Kerala, last week, Charu Nivedita was a huge draw, fielding questions from the audience about the style of his writing. Khanna and his co-translator Pritham K Chakravarthy read out passages from the novel, which is today, considered a pathbreaking work in Tamil literature. "I consider my novel as auto-fiction," Nivedita, told his audience at the Hay festival. "It is autobiography and fiction. I understand there is an auto-fiction movement in France," he added. The novel's transgressive narrative on sex, violence and low life, which broke the narrative structure in Tamil literature, came under fire from critics, who called it 'pornography'. Many other critics, however, have since called the novel a milestone in Tamil literature.

"My novel was like a guerrilla attack on the society," Charu says, who is angry with Dravidian politics and Brahminical indifference to Tamil culture. "Both have raped the Tamil language, which has shrunk and become superfluous," he fumes. "The members of Brahmin families talk Tamil only to vegetable vendors and their maids," says Charu. "The Dravidians consider Tamil Nadu's chief minister M.Karunanidhi as an artist. What is his claim to be an artist?"

Zero Degree is replete with phone sex, numerology, torture scenes and conversations in slum dwellings. "I wanted to free the chains imposed by the intelligentsia and the so-called culture wallahs from the Tamil language," explains Charu Nivedita, who published an internet novel in 2008 titled *Kaamarooba Kadhaigal,* which deals with internet addiction and cybersex. *Raasa Leela,* his popular novel, is based upon political oppression. "Being a writer in Tamil Nadu is like being a musician in the Taliban," says Charu. "The powerful and influential sections of Tamil society can't distinguish between eroticism and pornography or sexuality and vulgarity," says the author.

"My first novel was treated like a song of freedom by fellow writers in Tamil, which has a long tradition of understanding different literary traditions through translations from World Literature."

Charu Nivedita's childhood in Muslim-dominated Nagore, Tamil Nadu, which boasts of a Sufi tradition and its closeness to Karaikal, Pondicherry, which in turn has a strong Christian tradition, may have influenced his outlook towards society. "There was certainly an impact. I was growing up in a place full of cultural contradictions," he says. The contradictions in his life continue even today. Charu Nivedita, who worked in the Delhi administration issuing ration cards to its residents, writes in Malayalam journals more than in his own language.

Malayalam writer Paul Zacharia says in his foreword to the Malayalam translation of Zero Degree that the novel is "like an open experimental laboratory". "Amidst the smoke, noxious vapours, and beautiful imagery, I experienced a wondrous journey."

Charu Nivedita's own journey has only just begun.

* * *

I'M A FAN OF WILLIAM DALRYMPLE

Interviewed by Daniel Thimmayya

The New Indian Express

January 21, 2012

They say that Charu Nivedita is a man born of fierce passion and sardonic satire. One of Chennai's favourite literary sons, even this post-modern Tamil writer could not help but confess that he was 'excited' at being a part of the Jaipur Literature Festival 2012.

Touted as the biggest confluence of writers, poets, politicians, speakers and literary junkies to gather under one majestic roof on the continent, this has given the Exile author the opportunity to hobnob with some of the world's biggest names.

But despite sharing the literary space with the likes of Oprah Winfrey, Shashi Tharoor, Deepak Chopra and even Javed Akhtar, Charu's sights are set on one person primarily. "I'm a huge fan of William Dalrymple," he gushes. "Right from the time I read his In Xanadu, I've been hooked. I saw him when he came in this morning, but haven't spoken (to him) yet," he says and adds as a determined afterthought, "I will definitely meet him tomorrow!"

But when asked about what it was like to be around

so many writers and revolutionary essayists, Charu made a strange observation, "They're very decent... Such gentlemen. Most of them are so revolutionary on paper, but when I met them in person they are actually so docile and quiet," he says and reasons that this is a collateral damage that comes with increasing power and popularity. He begs to differ, "I'm going to kick up a storm during my session tomorrow."

JLF 2012 will see three sessions where Charu will be voicing his forthright views. "The major portion of my talks will be focused on censorship and dissent, besides handling one session with writer Bama Faustina called 'Two voices from Tamil' ", he told City Express from Jaipur. On how he came to be invited for this event that is expected to have close to 70,000 attendees at the Diggi Palace, he says, "My writing was really noticed during the Hay Festival earlier this year. The organizers were very impressed with my voice of dissent against politicians through fiction and word got around to the JLF organizers too."

But there's more: "So many Tamil writers are amazing writers but they cannot imagine coming to a place like this (JLF). Why? Simply because they do not publish their works in English," he reveals. "Most people here and across the world remember me for Zero Degree, because its satire and fire is maintained through translation."

* * *

AUTHOR'S PAROLE

Interviewed by Tishani Doshi

(An excerpt of this interview was published in The New Indian Express *on March 18, 2012 under the title* 'Addicted to Sex and Writing'.)

The first time I met Charu Nivedita was at the Hay Festival in Thiruvananthapuram in 2010. We shared a taxi from the airport into town. "I'm looking forward to this," he told me, "I've been holed up finishing a novel. It took me 16 days to write!" I didn't believe anyone could finish a book in 16 days, but then, I'd never met anyone like Charu before.

By his estimation Charu has written about 40 books: six are novels, the rest nonfiction (books on international literature, world cinema, music and translations). To write, he says he must be in a schizoid mode - "a state which does not have place for any audience, friends, or people with questions. I am the king there; God and the jester." Even to talk about his writing he has to enter this schizoid state, which is why he doesn't want to meet in person for this interview, even though we live in the same city.

Tishani Doshi

TD: How would you describe your work to an audience that doesn't know anything about you?

CN: Critics call me a subversive and a transgressive writer. Neither am I happy about these adjectives, nor do I approve of them. I do not have such intentions when I write. I don't think other writers too have such intendments. With what purpose did William Burroughs write *Naked Lunch*? I can say that the same creative process that was inherent in his four years of drug addiction while writing his experiences, is present in me too when I write. I have been exploring my body through my writings. Also, apart from saying my body is my writing, I constantly write about the fidgets and fervency of the female body. That is the reason my world is made up of women. That is the reason I dedicated my novel *Zero Degree* to Kathy Acker. I consider the writers who experimented with their body, my compatriots; writers such as Georges Bataille (*Story of The Eye*; *My Mother*), Marquis de Sade (*Philosophy in The Bedroom*, *120 Days of Sodom*) and Kathy Acker (*Blood And Guts in High School*; *Pussy, King of The Pirates*). Although I feel certain proximity with them, I experience boredom rather than enjoyment of the pleasure of their works. Their writing is not as fascinating as Mario Vargas Llosa. Hence I could say that my writing is a combination of Georges Bataille and Llosa. Currently, sans *Zero Degree*, when none of my works are available in English, this might sound like a tall claim. Soon, my other works will be available in English.

TD: How many books have you written to date?

CN: Could be 35 - 40. A number to be happy about in thirty five years of literary life. The adversity here is that only six of these books are novels and the rest are non-fiction. If you read my books, you will not find the difference between fiction and nonfiction. I was writing three serials in three prestigious magazines of Kerala, namely Madhyamam, Kala Koumudhi and Mathru Boomi. I do not know Malayalam. My Tamil articles were translated in Malayalam by my translator. One series was about Maghreb literature, the second was my novel *Raasa Leela* and the third, about various forms of music, ranging from Rai to Latin American. Even if they were swapped by mistake they wouldn't have created confusion, my friends would taunt. My distress is that at-least five of those 30 non-fictions could have become novels. Hence, I have stopped writing non-fiction. My first book, *Latin American Cinema: An Introduction* was published when I was 25. I was in Delhi then. The Indian movie buffs usually adored Satyajit Ray, Akira Kurosawa and the European cinema, whereas I was attracted towards Latin American films. I have talked a lot about directors like Jorge Sanjines and Glauber Rocha in that book, who are little known in India. I have written six books on Tamil, Hindi and European cinema. I have translated the works of writers like Maria Luisa Bombal, Arturo Uslar Pietri, Augusto Roa Bastos, Alejandra Pizarnik, Ronald Sukenik (His novel "*98.6*" is a great work), Rojelio Sinan, Oscar Lewis, Charles Bukowski, Radwa Ashour, Najwa Barakkat, Sahar Khalifeh, Nawal Al-Saadawi, Emile Nasrallah and Ghada Samman.

TD: When I met you in Kerala you had written a novel – the name? – you said you had written it in sixteen days. What was the reception to that novel and what have you been doing between now and then?

CN: The name of the novel is *Corpus*. Yes. I wrote it in almost two weeks (2010), as I had a concrete plot in my mind. I worked on this plot when I was relaxing in an Ayurvedic Center in Kerala. I was able to finish the novel as I did not have any work for two weeks. The novel talks about the anguish and torment of the body.

Let me explain. I had quit my postal department job due to desperate reasons, divorced and was starving along with my six year old daughter. It was a living hell for a 40 year old man to survive in a city like Madras with his kid. To survive, I picked pockets for a few years. After sometime I sold my semen in a semen bank, which was far worse than picking-pockets as I found it difficult to ejaculate when I masturbated. My body needs the perfect copulation for ejaculation. This numbness that is prevalent in my body might have been the result of my pick-pocketing years. I used to drink Oxtail soup every day, to bear the brunt of police beatings when I got caught. The nurse or the girl (I do not know how to term the girl who worked at the semen bank) would knock at the door shouting "Sir, you have taken plenty of time". During those days, I used to survive on rotten tomatoes.

Do you know how I quit being a pocket picker? It was an absurd situation. I bought a blade from a petty shop and got into a bus. When I tried taking the blade out, the packet was empty! I got down from the bus at T. Nagar Panagal Park. It was a hot summer afternoon. I was famished. I had had no food for three consecutive days. I ay down as I felt dizzy. I took a bite of the Durva grass nearby and vomited immediately. It had the stench of urine. Seeing a dog feasting on dried up human feces, I made my life changing decision. I agreed to act as a catamite to a doctor who was approaching me for sex. I have written everything in *Corpus*, my novel, which is under translation now.

After *Corpus*, I began with a long novel titled *Marginal Man*. Until *Marginal Man*, sex was an affliction to me. For the first time, sex transformed into a celebration for me in *Marginal Man*. It is a hedonistic novel. The imprisoned body gets liberated through sex. Mind becomes ecstatic. *Marginal Man* is my favorite among my six novels.

TD: Your mother tongue is Tamil but you are more popular in Kerala. Is that correct? How many languages have you been published in?

CN: The mother tongue factor still puzzles me. I think and write in Tamil. But, culturally, I don't think I am in Tamil Nadu. I consider myself as a French writer, writing in Tamil. Tamil Nadu has never accepted my writing. Kerala does. Although I do not know Malayalam, I have witnessed hundreds of people thronging to listen to my speeches. There is not a place I have never visited in Kerala. Be it a book release function, or the protest of the tribals, or an international film festival, the people consider me as an inseparable element. The reason is that, Kerala celebrates writers, whereas, it is Cinema in Tamil Nadu. I am keen on translating my novels into other languages.

Zero Degree is getting translated in French and Hindi. The English translation of *Corpus* is almost complete. *Marginal Man* and *Raasa Leela* in English, is on-going. I might not write in Tamil anymore. If the Tamils want to read me, let them translate it.

TD: What in your mind is the role of literature and books?

CN: The world is in chaos. Literature and books are the only factors that can save the world from disaster, I believe. Nothing can replace literature. Tamil Nadu has become philistine because they ignore literature. Just like how eyes are the light of the soul, literature is the light of mankind. The Tzarist Russia is an example. A society can identify its wilderness only through its literature. The writer cures the disease of the society. Mankind would have been extinct without literature. Just like Dostoyevsky was the hope of Tzarist Russia and Pablo Neruda, to Latin America, writers are the torch bearers of the society. They are the hope. Without Literature, man becomes an animal.

TD: Do you think that literature still serves a role in today's society given that it has to compete with the internet and television?

CN: The internet cannot be compared with television. It is but an extension of books. Without the internet we could have never read so many writers. Television is just a shadow. We can neither feel the shadow nor have a relationship with it. Nevertheless, it is not bad, just that people use it badly.

TD: Which are your favourite books? The books you go back to again and again?

CN: Shakespeare, Nikos Kazantzakis, Milorad Pavic, Verlaine, Arthur Rimbaud, Frederik Nietsche and many others. It is a long list.

And the Hymns of Azhwars (*Nalayira Divya Prabandam*), Bible and the Bhagavat Gita.

TD: What gives you the impetus to write a book – and when you begin – what is the process of writing – does it change?

CN: Certainly. My writing does change. I create my writing while in a schizoid mode where I am in a possessed state. The average moments of routine life are very little in my life. I think I disguise myself as a gentleman in those average moments. That's why I'm reluctant to give an interview and I prattle along when somebody asks me about my works. (This is why I proposed the interview through writing). My friends, without knowing the difference, question me often, "Seriously did you write these books? Or do you have a ghost writer?" Yes. It is a ghost. But my own. I will have to enter my schizoid state to talk about my writing. A state which does not have a place for any audience, people with questions or friends. I am the king there; the God and the jester. Plenty of factors create my schizoid state, beginning from the howling of Euripides' *Medea* to the news I read in the papers. A 43 year old teacher eloped with her 15 year old student. Her body's burning desire, agitates me to write another *Kamarooba Kadhaigal!*

My novel *Kamarooba Kadhaigal* is the most challenging work in my literary life. The novel is an account of the sexual life of teenage girls, witnessed deep down in their own world. I was 55 then, but transformed myself into a 30 year old and entered their world. They used to address me as 'da'. I have seen a girl's hands trembling like that of a drug addict, after sending five hundred text messages to her boyfriend on a single day. I came across a girl who had sexual relationships with four boys during the same span of time. They resembled female characters from Catherine Breillat's movies.

When I complete one of my novels, the next six months are spent in preparation for my next. In Tamil Nadu, one need not work hard for that as thousands of incidents happen right in front of your eyes and these incidents undergo an alchemical change in my private abode. It is impossible to explain what happens there.

The story creates the story. The text creates the text. It is a magic web, where I, the author and the text, create one another.

My novel *Raasa Leela* portrays the torments of the male body. In the mansions of Triplicane, Chennai, you could get to meet thousands of men who have not experienced sex in their entire lifetime. I had lived there. It's a world burning with the desire of lust. Between the age of 32 and 42, I had never touched a woman. It was a world devoid of women. It resembles the world of Erika Kohut, the character from Elfriede Gelinek's *Piano Teacher*.

In short, I transmigrate for each of my novels. Adi Sankara, who transmigrated to discover the meaning of sex when he faced Sarasavani's question, is my precedent in this regard.

TD: How do you tackle that famous "is it autobiographical" question when it comes to your fiction?

CN: Nobody has questioned me thus. Even if I disagree that it is not autobiographical, no one would believe it. What they miss to see is that I am not a single being. I have innumerable souls in me. This makes it difficult for me to tell up to what extent my works are autobiographical. Yet, I have never written without hints of autobiography. I envy writers like J.G. Ballard for that. I have always wanted to write a novel without this autobiographical touch. But since my life encompasses unexpected and adventurous incidents that are more interesting than a detective novel, my wish remains unfulfilled to this day.

TD: Could you describe to an English speaking audience what it means to work and write for a Tamil audience. What makes them different from other audiences? What are their strengths and weaknesses?

CN: You have caught me spot on, even when I tried to escape from your question about the reception to *Corpus*. Exile speaks about a writer's plight in Tamil Nadu, which is similar to living as an artist in a country of blind people, living as a musician in a country of deaf citizens and surviving as a goldsmith in a country of beggars.

The elixir of the Tamils is cinema. The writers in films are considered to be the only writers, which is why I request my friends not to introduce me as a writer, when in public. In case that happens, the immediate question I face is, "Which film are you currently writing?" Else, they ask me which police station I write at, as there is a post of a writer in every police station. You can never encounter a philistine society worse than Tamil Nadu in the entire world. You can witness the writers who write for *masala* films, being awarded the doctorate by famous universities here. In the bygone DMK regime, a vice chancellor announced that he was planning to translate former chief minister Karunanidhi's works in English, to be sent to the Nobel committee. Can you witness such a drollery anywhere else? If Kapil Sibal recites poetry in the north, he is ridiculed. But if Karunanidhi reads out his poetry, he is hailed as the heir of Elango Adigal (author of the Tamil classic, *Silappadhikaram*). Recently, a Tamil cinema lyricist has lamented in magazines that he has been insulted by his translators. Just because I can hit the golf ball, could I compare myself to Tiger Woods? These are my words from *Marginal Man*.

–

Recently a Tamil *masala* cinema (*masala* refers to Indian spice – you can imagine films like *Rambo*, *Commando*, *Double Impact* with few songs and dances by *saree* clad, semi nude women with a guy wearing leather jackets - climatic and weather conditions do not determine this attire) director was awarded with a honorary Doctorate. In the west, Che Guevara is considered a revolutionary, not the mighty Sylvester Stallone for his super-human stunts in cinema. In Tamil Nadu, the movie hero is a "Revolutionary leader", since he performs (of course with body doubles - not in romantic scenes) gravity defying stunts on screen. If it is Noam Chomsky there for a social scientist, here it is Mani Ratnam for Tamilians, since he offers good, easy solutions to deep rooted social, ethnic, economic, religious and divisive nationalistic problems in his cinemas. Kamal Haasan is the unofficial philosopher here due to his indefatigable pronouncement of philosophical quotes in cinema and in real life; the west is condemned with Michel Foucault for a Philosopher. ("I don't say god doesn't exist; I only say it would be good if he does.") Under such a circumstance, how can I hail myself as a writer? Pulp writers are present in all societies, but, only in Tamil Nadu, they are equals with the literary people. Mills & Boon and García Márquez are the same here.

Hypocrisy is the other issue of the Tamil people. I heard a very famous orator speak, "Remember, if cupid doesn't strike you in your twenties, something's very wrong with your body. If it strikes in your forties, then something's wrong with your mind". A thousand people applaud hearing this speech. What sort of country is this? Do we have to cut our dicks as soon as we turn forty? I have been writing in this cultural environment for the past 40 years. It is the same society in which a 40 year old school teacher elopes with a 15 year old student. Recently, a school principal has been arrested for sexually assaulting plenty of his students, for many years. The details which the female students provided exactly resembled a Marquis de Sade novel. If I write about these issues, I'm stamped as a porno writer. Now, I had stopped writing in Tamil and have started writing in English.

The other important issue is that there is no audience here. I roamed endlessly in the streets of Triplicane , carrying the manuscript of *Zero Degree*, 20 years ago. No publisher came forward to publish Zero Degree. I pledged my wife's *mangal sutra* (I don't believe in *mangal sutras* but my wife, Avanthika considers it sacred) to try and print it. But alas, I could never find a printer because they suspected my manuscript was something subversive and did not want to take a risk. And they were right. The English critics say Zero Degree is a subversive text like those of Kathy Acker or William Burroughs, but the Triplicane printers guessed rightly long before that *Zero Degree* was subversive without knowing a thing about Kathy Acker or William Burroughs.

I have been my publisher for all my books till I found a publisher some eight years back. When I published *Zero Degree*, it was not well received in Tamil Nadu. Here, writers are more conservative than the public. The sexual content in the novel was not acceptable to my fellow writers and it was totally rejected. (I liked their hatred because they are a Kafka gang and I don't like Kafka!) I have heard that Kathy Acker faced the same situation when she wrote and published in 70's and 80's.

Q. How do you tackle criticism of your work?

A. There is no criticism in Tamil Nadu. They just attack brutally. What is wrong in saying that I am addicted to sex and writing? Immediately they declare me to be a sex psycho. If Georges Bataille lived here, they would have hung him. College students complain to me that they face a heavy fine if they read me. I cannot name the colleges, as it is not an official fine. Female students write to me that my novels are read clandestinely.

In Tamil Nadu, the intelligentsia practices cultural fascism, more than the common people. Twenty years ago, I directed and acted in a stage play, named 'The Night show' (*Rendaam Aattam*), in a theatre festival at Madurai. Those days, the blue films (bit films, they are called) were shown only during the night shows, and hence the title. The drama was based on the Forum Theatre concept of Augusto Boal and Antonin Artaud's concept of Theatre of Cruelty. The play had a few homosexual scenes. But the scenes were so stylish, and I had structured them as beautiful dance movements. (I am a huge fan of Udhaya Shankar). We were attacked when the drama was only half way through. The properties of the play were broken. The female member of the play too, was attacked. The attackers were none other than drama scholars, who had doctorates. The cry of a professor, 'You are insulting the theatre', still lingers in my ears. Surprisingly, an old spectator praised me, saying that he is a Gandhian, who had been imprisoned during the freedom struggle. When I asked about a Gandhian supporting a homosexual play, he said that he does not support my view, but then he supports the freedom of expression. He remembered the olden days, when they were stoned while staging plays against untouchability. That Gandhian was supported by a movement. Since I am a lonely man, I withdrew myself from the play, fearing my life.

Two decades back, the Latin American writers were exiled. Julio Cortazar lived in exile, in France. Here, no one is exiled, but they insult by naming me a sex psycho in the magazines. Also, writing in Tamil is similar to writing in a diary. Even though I am a famous writer, my books never sell beyond a thousand copies. I have written a lot about Jean Paul Sartre and Michel Foucault. I have translated Sartre's short story, The wall and his novella, Intimacy and I doubt if at least a hundred readers would have read it. I have written about Ulrike Ottinger and Catherine Breillat in detail. But now, I think it is a waste of time.

I have decided henceforth that I will write only in English. I am an introvert. I don't go out much or socialize. I have two huge dogs, a Labrador and a Great Dane, who take up most of my time. I work like a machine. Once a week, I go to the pub with some friends. Though writing does not pay, I have friends who take care of me. I have a kind of fanatic reader following. (They have formed a Readers Forum too on Facebook). They say that my writing mesmerizes. Well, I don't know!

* * *

'ARTISTS MUST GO BEYOND IDEOLOGIES'

Interviewed by T.N. Shaji

Education Insider

July 2012

S: What's your opinion on creativity and education?

CN: Creativity and education are poles apart in the contemporary education system, which focuses on improving knowledge rather than wisdom, an integral element of creativity. Youths graduating from institutions are like plastic buckets being cloned out from a moulding machine. This should alert every Indian.

S: Do you think there is a general aversion among people to read fiction nowadays? Does that have anything to do with the technological explosion?

CN: Today's youth lack reading habit. The primary reason for this is that they have taken to the disadvantages of technical growth, instead of advantages. They are addicted to video games, social networking sites, mobile phones and gadgets. Games like RapeLay, a molestation simulation game, are popular among the youth. The accusing finger here has to be pointed at the system of education, which has been turned into a horse race that gives them mental stress and physical pressure. The youth seldom read fiction in India. Only implementation of fundamental reforms in the education sector as in the western countries, can bring about a progression from this pathetic state.

S: How would you describe your novel Zero Degree to someone who has not read any of your works?

CN: My novel *Zero Degree* could shock the readers who have not read my other works. But it can give them a sense of proximity if they are familiar with transgressive writings like that of Kathy Acker and Cristina Peri Rossi. Also, the primary difference between Indian novels and *Zero Degree* would be the universal nature of plot, which surpasses the Indian boundaries. And it doesn't possess any Indianness or the life of the Tamils. Unlike the conventional course adopted by the writers in India, where even anthropology and autobiography are considered to be part of literature, this novel takes the road less travelled.

S: Will you explore existentialism, deconstruction etc. in your future books?

CN: I never create my fiction based on any existing 'isms'. I like concepts and ideologies, like that of Jorge Luis Borges, whose works have the components of structuralism, though he never had the intention to create such components. An artist should go beyond ideologies and concepts. Friedrich Wilhelm Nietzsche, Michel Foucault and Roland Barthes have made a great impact on me, and that remains the under stream of whatever I have written and would write henceforth.

S: What are you reading right now? Are there any authors

(living or dead) that you would name as influences?

CN: In world literature, nobody attracts me like Shakespeare. I read him often. In my opinion, a master is one who can attract his readers time and again. There are indeed two authors whom I read frequently - Nikos Kazantzakis and Serbian writer Milorad Pavić. If the writing of Kazantzakis can be categorized as modern epic, Pavić creates a maze in his writings. These are my two favourites.

Apart from these two, the contemporary Arabic literature is at the helm now, surpassing Latin American and European literature. I could readily list at least fifteen writers, who are well qualified for the Nobel Prize, from Morocco and Algeria. I have read the works of writers like Tahar Ben Jelloun (Morocco), recipient of the prestigious Dublin Impac Award, Mohammed Berrada (Morocco), Assia Djebar and Ghada Samman (Lebanon), to name a few. The best is Abdul Rahman Munif (Saudi Arabia), who can be called the Dostoyevsky of the 20th century. But it is depressing to see Arabian literature not getting its due when compared with Latin American and European literature.

I forgot to name a writer who had influenced me. I have been influenced by European cinema and anybody who is familiar with European cinema can easily make out the influence of Jean-Luc Godard in my writings.

S: Which is the book that influenced your life the most? And how?

CN: More than books, people influence me; everyday life influences me. Even today, I read in newspapers that a 14 year old murdered an old lady to buy himself a Playstation, which kindled many questions in my mind, probing our life today. Such an episode in a Western country would have caused chaos throughout the nation. But in India, these incidents are a part of everyday life. Similar news gets published everyday, which makes us question factors like our education system and the way the children are brought up. But nobody is worried here; India has become a country for the elites and the upper class.

S: Name your five favourite books and tell me why you like them.

CN: 1.) Che Guevara's Bolivian Diary: The book made me think about living not just for myself, but for the sake of others.

2.) *Zorba the Greek* (Nikos Kazantzakis): The book made me realise that life as a genius, is not as useful as enjoying life. This book made me a hedonist.

3.) *Dictionary of Khazars* (Milorad Pavić): The book which taught me the limitless possibilities of fiction writing. One can keep reading it countless times.

4.) *The Mahabharata*: It makes me wonder if it is humanly possible to write such a book.

5.) *Meeting the Remarkable Men* (George Ivanovich Gurdjieff): The book proved to me that the modern thought process based on mere rational thinking was wrong and there are other ways of perceiving reality.

S: Tell me about your first job, and the inspiration for your writing, and any funny details that enlivened your page.

CN: In India, a doctor can live his life as a doctor. An engineer, a teacher, a goldsmith or any other professional can do his job and survive. But a writer is not that lucky. Literature would never give him his bread. Popularity - yes; But food - A big no. This realization made me take up a government job in my younger days. I worked for 20 years in three different departments. My tenure of 10 years with the Ration Department in Delhi was an interesting experience. I have written about these, in my novel *Rasa Leela*, in detail.

S: You said, "My writing is nothing but brush strokes of a person trying to escape from hell". Can you elaborate?

CN: Life is nothing but hell in Third World Countries. I flee from these tortuous nightmares only through my writings. In short, I could say that I am postponing my suicide through my writings.

S: Do you make any conscious effort to break the rules of society?

CN: I do not have any agenda while I write. It is an act of swinging between a schizoid state and creativity. I try to transform this schizoid state into art. Other than doing so, I never think about society or its rules. When I don't think about them how can I talk about breaking them? A writer is someone who transcends the boundaries of time, country and race - he becomes immortal and in doing so, is the equivalent to God, which is why social norms mean nothing to him. Once at Mahatma Gandhi University, Kottayam, while answering a question from a student about how I write, I replied impulsively, "I write as a bird flies".

S: You are a successful author. Do you think it is viable to be a full-time writer?

CN: Success does not bring money. A writer's job is one of the lowest paid in the world. My friends take good care of me. Hence, I am free from the problems faced by Kafka or Rimbaud. I completed my 700 page novel *Raasa Leela*, sitting in the bar of a five-star hotel in Chennai. One of my friends bore the expenses. As long as I have friends like these, I can concentrate on my writings, without worrying about the miseries of mundane life.

Opinion in newspapers

On the popularity of charuonline.com/blog

Deccan Chronicle

June 12, 2008

Controversial Tamil writer Charu Nivedita's charuonline. com has got a traffic rank of 232,947, a previously unheard of rank for any Tamil writer's website. This came to light after Alexa, a web traffic information company, ranked the Tamil writer's site as one of the most popular Tamil sites. Alexa's ranking is considered a yardstick to measure the popularity of various websites across the world. "I am happy that my website is gaining popularity among Tamils across the world. I update my website almost every day," said Charu Nivedita. "I am writing more about Arab literature on my website now," said the writer.

* * *

God and I

(As told to Arun Janardhanan)

I always communicate with God through my writings. In my childhood, I was a true believer of God. Later I started my sojourn with Marxism. I was not a non-believer; but an agnostic.

I have always engaged myself with this ontological question through my writings; I have travelled through the worlds of Sufis and Zen Buddhists. I always keep religion at a distance because religion and the search for God are two different things. I have realized that there is no relation of mine with God and religion.

But I always converse with God and was looking for a witness like the Sufi saint Khwaja Shamsuddin Hafiz (1326-1390) who lived in Iran. He had waited for 40 years to have an experience of God. In 2005, I had an experience with God. I was in Champs Elysees, Paris. The day was December 22nd. One of my friends told me about St. Lourdes. "But you can't simply go and visit that place. She will call you if you deserve it," he said. The next day I was about to return to India but suddenly an unknown reader of my writings came to my room and asked me to cancel the trip in order to visit his village Lourdes, near the France-Spain border. I visited the Church of St. Lourdes on Christmas Eve and it was a spiritual experience. The message from Shirdi Baba also influenced my life spiritually. Silence helps me communicate with the concept of God. This silence is the power of my writings.

* * *

On his works that appear on the internet first and in print later.

Times of India

January 1, 2010

Charu Nivedita who runs his own website is enjoying his www avatar. "If an incident happens in the morning, I am able to broadcast my response by afternoon to my readers across the world. I don't have to depend on any magazine," he says. Nearly 20 of Charu Nivedita's books carrying content that first appeared on the internet are out in the market.

"My internet columns are print-ready. I write them keeping in mind the fact that they are going to appear in print later," he says.

* * *

On the difference between erotic writing and porn

The New Indian Express

August 4, 2010

Charu Nivedita believes that eroticism is the pulse of life. His works deal with painful eroticism. "The erotic writings of Marquis de Sade and Elfriede Jelinek have inspired my works. Erotic literature finds its roots in the age of Sangam and Kambar poetry. It has been reported that even Avvaiyyar, in one of her poems, mentioned that she wanted to sip palm wine with King Adhiyaman." Charu is an encyclopedia on erotic literary works. He shares, "Soundarya Lahiri and Andal's Thiruppavai, belong to the class of spiritual erotic writing. These days, there is a repression of writers who deal with eroticism." He also goes to say, "Real eroticism involves appreciating sex. One is branded a 'porno writer', even if the piece deals only with eroticism."

Charu also agrees that the pornification is a result of the influence of Victorian morality. He smiles, "Today, poets write porn. There is no tinge of eroticism in it."

* * *

My favourite books

Tehelka

November 13, 2010

Of late, Sharmistha Mohanty's *New Life* really moved me. A story of a woman from Kolkata, it delves into the conflict between eastern and western cultures. Another interesting book is Tahar Ben Jelloun's *This Blinding Absence of Light*, a story of prisoners surviving in the dark. Besides these, I have some favourites that include Nikos Kazantzakis' *Zorba the Greek* and *Report to Greco*. Both books argue that the root cause for violence is a spiritual vacuum in life. I also liked Rory Stewart's *The Places in Between*, on his journey through Afghanistan after the departure of the Taliban.

* * *

On item songs and rape

Deccan Chronicle

January 5, 2013

"Our young men are desensitized by their consumerist attitudes where they consider women as a sexual commodity. The pelvic movements and gyrations in our cinema songs can challenge blue films and the viewer age spectrum is from a baffling three-year-old toddler to a 90 year nonagenarian," says writer Charu Nivedita.

* * *

On the portrayal of a minor girl in a liplock scene in Mani Ratnam's *Kadal*

Deccan Chronicle

23 January, 2013

Question: The female lead in one of the most celebrated Tamil films, Kadal, was a grade nine student. The female protagonist of a yet to be released Tamil film is a 16-year-old girl, who is seen locking lips in the film's trailer.

Charu: "It doesn't project a great picture. Awareness about forbidding the casting of underage girls in films must be fast spread. Even the Censor Board, which ruthlessly chops off common slang, turns a blind eye to this dangerous trend."

* * *

On children being allowed to watch 'A' certified films.

Deccan Chronicle

February 4, 2013

Charu: "My concern primarily is that in most places, children below 18 are allowed to watch 'A' certified films. There must be a strict vigil on this."

Question: However, this also raises the question about actors flashing their six packs while uttering popular punchy one-liners. Would such representation also be scrapped from television?

Charu: "Be it a man or a woman, nudity cannot be termed vulgar, as it is purely contextual."

* * *

On translations

Economic Times

December 15, 2013

"There is no cross-cultural bridge between states here. While you could find [Mario Vargas] Llosa, [Jorge Luis] Borges and (Gabriel Garcia) Marquez even in Tamil, you cannot find many Bengali or Hindi books in Tamil or English," says Charu Nivedita.

* * *

On hero worship in India

Al Jazeera

March 21, 2014

Charu Nivedita says, "Civic and political changes have influenced popular tastes in the state. South Indians have an emotional nature that can be naive. The influx of pulp cinema, supported by a political and an entertainment culture, has led to an erosion of its classical aesthetics. Cinema has contributed to a culture of deification of film stars."

* * *

On the Beep song controversy

India Today

December 13, 2015

Charu Nivedita blasted Anirudh and Simbu for the untimely release of the song. The writer condemned them for releasing such a song during a time when the whole of Chennai and a few other districts were suffering from the flood waters. He further stated that he has no problem with the word, since it is like any other word in usage.

* * *

On Ilaiyaraaja's verbal abuse towards a journalist.

India Today

December 18, 2015

Charu Nivedita, in his Facebook post said that Ilaiyaraaja could have avoided answering the question if he didn't want to. He further said that this type of an outburst was not only a physical brawl but also violence.

* * *

On the Beep song controversy

The Hindu

December 22, 2015

Charu Nivedita questioned the very need for such a composition. "The very basis of eve-teasing comes from youth being influenced by what they see in popular culture and how lightly it is represented. Apart from being extremely offensive to women, songs like these influence a society to act vulgar," he said.

He further added, "The mindset of relegating women to specific roles within households and discriminating against their capabilities is what comes through in songs like this. At an individual level, we should introspect and raise our voices against such misogyny and vulgarity."

* * *

On Na. Muthukumar's early demise

The Times of India

August 24, 2016

Writer Charu Nivedita sees more practical underpinnings to the situation. He says the lack of recognition for a writer in Tamil society is the reason why they waste away their lives while still young.

"Writers don't get the money or recognition for their work. When they see that there is no recognition for what they do, they get depressed and take up habits like drinking," he says.

As someone who has been consistently vocal about how writers and poets are neglected in society, Charu Nivedita says: "The writer doesn't exist in Tamil society."

"A friend who joined a political party said that he did not get any recognition even after writing for long, so he took up politics. Look at the extent to which writers get demoralised. Either they drink themselves to death or they join mainstream cinema or politics and become morally corrupt," he says.

* * *

On pen-names

The Times of India

October 16, 2016

Choosing a name is like recreating a personality, as it does away with caste and religious identities, feels writer Charu Nivedita. Though adopted out of necessity - being a government clerk – the fictional name was a reflection of his writing. "I adopted the name of Nivedita from Swami Vivekananda's disciple Sister Nivedita, as I was writing spiritual articles for a magazine as a teenager. The other part of my name was in remembrance of the communist revolutionary Charu Majumdar. The pseudonym stands for the rebel character and my spiritual inclination," says the 63-year-old who also wrote as Muniyandi to publish novels dealing with sexuality and incest.

In the years where he worked at the postal department in Chennai, the author had been reprimanded for pursuing his creative ambitions, denied increment and forced to resign in 2001. His experience of the oppressive nature of bureaucracy was documented in his novel *Rasa Leela*. The author was inspired to take a female name from the renowned writer Sujatha, also a government staffer who used his wife's name. He feels that stringent bureaucracy is a reflection of society. "Tamil psyche is a bit conservative and this shows in all aspects of life."

* * *

Print or Ebook?

Deccan Chronicle

January 9, 2017

However, the bigger debate here is on why these writers move back to print media, when they have established themselves online. Charu Nivedita, one of the prominent writers, reasons, "Though they have thousands of followers online, printed books always have a sort of glamour which makes them shift to the conventional medium. Call it superstitious belief but these online writers feel that publishing a book makes them proper writers! Maybe after 100 years, when there is a paperless society, a complete shift might happen."

He adds, "I published my book, Morgue Keeper, a short story collection, online. I now regret the decision because it has not been recognized by anyone. If it had been published as a hard copy it would have been read. So, even in this technology-driven world, online books are not taken into account like printed ones. That's the reason writers still go after print."

But do these writers attract new readers or are the buyers of their books only their online followers? Charu asserts, "Unfortunately, the readership becomes stagnant. Conventional readers clearly don't read these books, and this new trend is only running parallel and separately. The fault also lies with the writers because they produce only flash fiction and lack in-depth reading and effort."

* * *

Speaking in the Mother Tongue.

Deccan Chronicle

February 21, 2017

Charu Nivedita, believes that the only way to get people back to speaking their mother tongues properly, is a shake-up of the education system. He says, "In the west, it is necessary for a student in France or Germany to study and clear certain levels of French and German respectively, whereas in our country, we always have the option of choosing not to study our mother tongues, and taking up foreign languages. Our education system is killing our mother languages, and we need to change the way we look at our language policy."

Charu adds – "In our state, during the recent Jalikattu protests, which were about fighting for Tamil identity, one could notice how more than half of the protesters didn't know any Tamil. If we don't take steps to change our educational system, there is a chance that Tamil could turn into the Aramaic language, the language that was spoken by Jesus Christ and now has only 3,000 people who can speak it."

* * *

Pawternity Leave

Deccan Chronilce

April 17, 2017

(In an unprecedented move in the country, HarperCollins

India is granting five paid leaves for their employees, who are adopting dogs, cats or any other pets as part of their family. The paid holidays, called 'Pawternity leave', are provided for a person to bond with his/her pet during the initial days after the adoption. Though many companies in the west grant such leaves, HarperCollins is the first one to come up with the idea in India.)

Charu Nivedita, who owns two dogs himself, says, "It is a good initiative, no doubt. But there are some fundamental changes that need to be made first — the attitude of humans towards animals. Things like pelting stones at dogs, throwing them from the third floor, etc., should stop."

"The aversion to dogs and cats is so strong in the society that people who have pets are not given houses for rent. Apartments have strict rules against having pets. Even if you are ready to shell out more money, house owners turn you down. These are the first things that have to be addressed. Empathy towards animals should be natural," Charu adds, signing off.

* * *

photo credit: prabhu kalidas

Charu Nivedita is a postmodern Tamil writer born in 1953. He was born and raised in a slum until the age of 18, worked in the government services and survived as a wanderer. Since his writings are transgressive in nature, he is branded as a pornographic writer. For a longtime he was writing clandestinely under the pseudonym 'Muniyandi'.

He was selected as one among 'Top Ten Indians of the Decade 2001-2010' by the Economic Times. He is inspired by Marquis de Sade, Georges Bataille and Andal. His columns appear in ArtReview Asia, The Asian Age and several other magazines.

He lives a reclusive life in Chennai, with his wife, two dogs and a cat.

unfaithfully yours